The *Seinfeld* Universe

N.Y.C.
6/30/07

The *Seinfeld* Universe

The Entire Domain

NEW AND UPDATED

Greg Gattuso

A CITADEL PRESS BOOK
PUBLISHED BY CAROL PUBLISHING GROUP

For Granny and Pop,
who taught me how to play poker.
And Mom,
who raised me good.

A Citadel Press Book
Published by Carol Publishing Group
Citadel Press is a registered trademark of Carol Communications, Inc.
Editorial, sales and distribution, and rights and permissions inquiries should be
   addressed to Carol Publishing Group, 120 Enterprise Avenue, Secaucus, N.J. 07094
In Canada: Canadian Manda Group, One Atlantic Avenue, Suite 105, Toronto,
   Ontario M6K 3E7

Carol Publishing Books may be purchased in bulk at special discounts for sales
promotion, fund-raising, or educational purposes. Special editions can be created to
specifications. For details, contact Special Sales Department, Carol Publishing Group,
120 Enterprise Avenue, Secaucus, N.J. 07094.

Manufactured in the United States of America
10 9 8 7 6 5 4 3 2 1

Library of Congress Cataloging-in-Publication Data

Gattuso, Greg.
       The Seinfeld universe : the entire domain / Greg Gattuso.
          p.   cm.
       "A Citadel Press book."
       ISBN 0-8065-2001-9 (pbk.)
       1. Seinfeld.   I. Title.
PN1992.77.S4285G38   1996
791.45'72—dc20   95-48055
                                                         CIP

Contents

Contents

Preface

"Blessed is he who expects nothing, for he shall never be disappointed."

—Jonathan Swift

There are no words to the *Seinfeld* theme song.

No sixty-second lyrical introduction of the plot, the characters, or the setting. Nothing to tip off the newcomer as to what he or she is in for over the next twenty-two minutes.

No ditty about a talking horse, castaways, or a bar where everybody knows your name.

Come to think of it, there are no real instruments in the theme song either. Just an amalgam of synthesized horns, a digitized slap-bass, a keyboard thing, and a series of orchestrated sighs, gasps, and lip pops. In other words, it's merely a loosely associated group of elements that somehow, when combined in the right amount, and in the proper sequence, makes sense. The same could apply to the *Seinfeld* show itself.

Seinfeld, as most of us know, is the situation comedy about nothing. Or, it's about everything. It's about life's biggest challenges, or life's most minuscule annoyances. It's really about . . . ah, forget it.

There are few people in the United States who are not already acquainted with Jerry, George, Elaine, and Kramer. Every week more than 30 million Americans tune in to see what TV's most recognizable New Yorkers will do next. Or, what they won't do.

Seinfeld is based on the principle that people's everyday lives are boring. So boring, in fact, that watching a half-hour of television is more interesting than living a half-hour of one's life.

Sure, that would seem to apply to a police drama, where New York's Finest can investigate a homicide, round up the killer, and turn him over to the courts, where he is tried, convicted, and sent to prison—all in one hour.

But what about a show where even the characters are bored?

And speaking of Jerry, George, Elaine, and Kramer, there's nothing particularly likable about them, explained the show's namesake, "except that they kind of remind you of yourself. That's their only redeeming quality."

To the uninitiated, the characters seem to lack appeal. Jerry Seinfeld notes, "they're incredibly selfish and conniving. They will even trick each other, their closest friends, for the basest of goals, usually money or sex."

The first character is Jerry Seinfeld. He's the ringleader, a comedian who works occasionally, usually at clubs not far from his apartment on the Upper West Side of Manhattan. When he's not working, he goes on dates, goes to the dry cleaner, or goes shopping.

"I actually only have three friends," Jerry confesses in "The Pool Guy." "I really can't handle any more."

Jerry's best friend, George Costanza—short-tempered, jealous, and petty—drops by the apartment to tell Jerry news. Only sometimes is the news classified as "good."

Elaine Benes is Jerry's ex-girlfriend. Her greatest feat is already behind her—breaking up with Jerry and managing still to be friends with him. One gets the sense that she should have no trouble in life. After all, she's independent, smart, charming, beautiful, and manages to hold well-paying (if dull) nine-to-five jobs. Yet she's stuck in life with the lot of them.

Jerry's neighbor, Cosmo Kramer, lives at least half his life in Jerry's apartment, where he borrows things, watches TV, eats, and stares at naked women across the street. He has no visible means of support, except that every now and then he gets a job—as anything from a fashion model to a department-store Santa to a revival-moviehouse manager. Mostly, he's an entrepreneur whose crazy ideas sometimes pay off.

The characters don't cook much, if at all. The gang eats out almost every episode, for reasons integral to the plots, which even the star describes as "a lot of coffee, a lot of lunches and dinners, a lot of swinging, and a lot of hanging."

Since they first hit the airwaves in the summer of 1989, Jerry and the gang have drunk a lot of coffee. They have also revolutionized television and made a social statement about how we look at each other and how we look at life. Now that the show is syndicated to every major market in the United States (and carried by cable and satellite to every corner of the globe), one presumes that *Seinfeld* will be ingrained in popular culture for years, and more likely decades, to come.

One of the challenges of writing an unauthorized book is chronicling the lives of your subjects (and analyzing their art) without their input. For this book, I studied hundreds of previously published articles about *Seinfeld* and watched dozens of videocassettes to present a fair and accurate account of the people and events that shaped this most unique show. Clearly, this book would not be what it is without the work of those journalists lucky enough to have met and interviewed the show's cast and crew. Whatever questions were left over I brought to a number of TV experts, comedy aficionados, and *Seinfeld* superfans—whether in person, over the phone, or via the Internet. These people, along with my talented editor, Carrie Nichols Cantor, have my profound thanks. (Leave this part in, Carrie.)

Occasionally, dates and facts were disputed, and publicists' accounts of the truth clashed with other publicists (or common sense). In these instances, I had no choice but to use old-fashioned judgment.

When I founded *Nothing: The Newsletter for Seinfeld Fans* in 1993, my goal was to produce the kind of fanzine that I, as a *Seinfeld* fan, would want to read (and, of course, buy). The same goes for this book; for only if the fans at the proverbial water coolers across America (and throughout the world) enjoy this offering will it truly have been worth the effort.

Now, if you'll excuse me, I'm going to the fridge for a Snapple. . . . These pretzels are making me thirsty.

The Show's the Thing

When NBC executives approached Jerry Seinfeld in 1988 to develop a show of his own, he was short on ideas. All he knew was that he didn't want to do a traditional sitcom. He turned to Larry David, an acquaintance and fellow stand-up on the New York comedy scene. David had been a writer-performer on ABC's *Fridays* and a writer for NBC's *Saturday Night Live*. Although he had the TV experience, David's career had been in low gear for some time. Yet Seinfeld, who was hot at the time, remembered David as a "comedian's comedian," who cracked up comics (and sometimes audiences) with his angst-ridden doomsday humor.

It was Larry who came up with the concept of Jerry as a comedian in New York City. The show, he proposed, would be about Jerry's everyday life and how it fueled the comic's stand-up act. While they differed in their comedy styles (David often came off angry and bitter, as opposed to Jerry's amused and annoyed), they both hated "homogenized" comedy shows and agreed that the show would be theirs with no compromises.

"We wanted the show to be about those idiotic conversations we have all the time," said David, who has more than forty *Seinfeld* writing or cowriting credits.

The idea of building a show around a comedian is not new. Bob Newhart did it in 1972 with his third stab at prime time television, *The Bob Newhart Show*. Newhart played Bob Hartley, a psychiatrist who, like the comic himself, observed weird goings-on in life, in his office, and among his neighbors in the Emmy-winning comedy.

The pilot episode of *The Seinfeld Chronicles* (later renamed *Seinfeld*), introduced Jerry, his best friend, George, and an eccentric neighbor, Kramer, who supposedly had not left his home in ten years (and owned a dog!). The story, about a female friend who can't find a hotel room and asks to stay at Jerry's place, was bent to fit the comic's stand-up material. As the show began to take form, however, Jerry would customize his monologue to reflect the plot of each episode.

Much of the material on *Seinfeld* has come from Jerry's and Larry's personal lives. Both have a comedic "third eye" that constantly scans the universe for comic fodder. Jerry's material goes into his stand-up act. David's goes into what has been called by *Seinfeld* insiders "Larry's magic treasure chest of notebooks." Even if one were to access the private comedy reserves of Seinfeld and David, it is doubtful he or she could fuse the elements into a television script as masterfully as they two have done. Yet Jerry credits Larry as the major force behind the show.

"He has, more than me, created this enterprise," Seinfeld said. "My skill has been to help him interpret his ideas. He filters things through me. I contribute lines and jokes."

Nevertheless, it *is* called *Seinfeld*.

Jerry Seinfeld plays Jerry Seinfeld, a comedian living in New York City and trying to pass the hours between shows. Like the real Jerry, TV Jerry (as he's called on the set) is single, thin, and neat. He loves baseball and fast cars. "His whole life revolves around Superman and cereal," his best friend once observed on the show.

"I am the guy," Jerry told Barbara Walters, referring to his TV double. "First of all, I'd say we look a lot alike. It's a strange thing to be that public. I mean, people really know me now. I can't act—that's it."

Most importantly, Jerry is the center of the *Seinfeld* universe. His apartment is where people meet. Where stories are exchanged. Where schemes are hatched. And the place where women often declare, "I'm leaving!"

Jerry Seinfeld and Larry David have said that there were no "second choices" for the rest of the cast. George was the first to be signed. David recalled seeing Jason Alexander's videotaped reading and saying "That's the guy." Alexander did another reading in Los Angeles, but at that point it was just a formality for studio execs. Michael Richards was also a first choice. He had known Larry since *Fridays* and Jerry through his various TV, movie, and stand-up gigs. Julia Louis-Dreyfus never even auditioned for the part of Elaine. David, having worked with her at *SNL*, recommended Jerry meet her over a bowl of cereal.

"I responded to them on a personal level," Jerry told an interviewer. "I like these people, so the chances of them liking each other and liking me were higher than if some casting agent just goes, 'Well, they're the best actor, and I want a blonde and we need a tall guy.' You put them together and it's not going to work. I picked them the way I pick my friends."

King George

If Jerry is suited to watching his dates hurry out of his apartment, then it is only fitting that his best friend be George Costanza, a man whose dates usually end with a firm "Get out!"

One wonders why Jerry and George have been friends for so long—since their days together in high school and college. On the surface, there is very little to like about George. He's a pathological liar and a hypochondriac—a man with more worries than even Felix Unger of *The Odd Couple*. He has no self-respect. He eats peanut butter with his index finger and urinates in public showers. He tells a lie and then opts to build more lies rather than come clean. A doctor on the show once diagnosed George as "a sick person. An immature person with no regard for wasting other people's time."

Yet somehow George represents the everyman in us—falling somewhere between Jerry (a handsome, successful bachelor who makes a living out of having fun) and Kramer (a hipster doofus who has no obligations and no apparent way of paying his rent). That leaves the large middle of the male population to identify with George: short, bald, bespectacled, battling the bulge, often unemployed, and cheap (when he has money), with few friends and fewer interests. In these tough times, it is George with whom audiences can form a bond—the one who gets a day-long adrenaline rush out of a perfect parking spot, hailing a cab, or making good time on a car trip.

"George is not a loser," explained *Seinfeld* writer-producer Larry Charles. "People inaccurately pigeonhole him. He's struggling, but he's definitely not a loser."

Perhaps it is because George is so well defined that he is the easiest to write for. He is the most plausible character to become the victim of embarrassing—even bizarre—situations. He schemes and lies when honesty is called for. And although he holds philosophical discussions over coffee with Jerry, they are both oblivious to the big picture.

"As urban and sophisticated as Jerry and George seem, they're so in the dark about so many things," noted Peter Mehlman, another writer-producer.

George wears the worst clothes on the show. It's not that they're so terribly out of style— or that the others are particularly in style. But George's clothes are remarkably unremarkable. While Jerry's attire is neat, Elaine's is yuppie-chic, and Kramer's is the garage-sale-vintage look, George dresses like "the rest of us"— sweatpants, jeans, baggy shirts, and formless coats. No wonder Mr. Blackwell once named George

Sweet charity: Jason lends a hand at Comic Relief 6. (Vinnie Zuffante/Star File)

Thank God for *Fridays*

Although it is unfairly dismissed as a *Saturday Night Live* rip-off, *Fridays*, ABC's early-eighties comedy and music show, should at least be remembered as the place that gave some *Seinfeld* stars their first crack at national exposure.

It was the show where Michael Richards and Larry David worked together, along with future *Seinfeld* writers Larry Charles and Elaine Pope. *Fridays* cast member Melanie Chartoff popped up in "The Fire" as the woman George failed to impress with his display of leadership during a birthday-party emergency. Likewise, Bruce Mahler played a loose-lipped rabbi in "The Postponement."

Richards is most remembered for his "Battle Boy" character, an overgrown, helmet-wearing kid whose backyard exploits with toy soldiers and tanks usually ended up with a blazing fire. Richards's other popular character, Dick, a suave, chain-smoking (and sometimes roller-skating) bachelor who came on to women in bars, is currently being resurrected for a Castle Rock movie.

Larry David, who also wrote for the show, could write and perform everything from dark comic satire to the purely absurd. In an example of the former, he played one of the founding fathers in a skit that found them in a late-night cram session to finish the U.S. Constitution. David's character (who was not identified) was wary of giving citizens the right to bear arms and wondered if someday society would change into one where citizens go crazy and shoot each other. The other founding fathers convinced David's character that if Americans did start to act this crazy, they could always amend the Constitution. David agreed to leave the right to bear arms in the document, reluctantly.

David provided much simpler humor in a Jewish version of the 1980s TV show *That's Incredible*, called *That's Meshugge*. In the sketch, David played one of two daredevil rabbis who rode a motorcycle through a giant "flaming bagel of death" and then through a wall of matzoh. David appears occasionally on *Seinfeld*. He played Frank Costanza's caped lawyer in

Those were the days: Larry David and Michael Richards rehearsing a sketch for *Fridays* in the early eighties. (© 1995 Capital Cities/ABC)

"The Chinese Woman" and a newsstand owner in "The Gum."

Fridays, like *SNL*, was inconsistent, with comedy and musical performances succeeding on a hit-or-miss basis each week.

Perhaps the most memorable moment on *Fridays* was an on-air fight between one of the show's producers and guest star Andy Kaufman, which still has people wondering if it was a publicity stunt.

to his list of the worst-dressed people on TV ("He's a total bag man"—whatever that means). His tuxedo is too tight. His one nice suit was stolen (the replacement made a swooshing noise when he walked).

Why would Jerry want to hang around with a guy like this? Despite their differences, Jerry and George share a view of the world. Who else but George would appreciate the fact that two of Jerry's vomit streaks (that is, spans of time without "refunding") ended on the same date—exactly thirteen years apart? Perhaps it is because George is so pathetic: no matter how bad life gets for Jerry, he can say to himself, "At least I'm not like George."

Maybe that's why *Seinfeld* fans were so relieved in 1994's "The Opposite," when George turned around his life as a loser to become a front-office executive with the New York Yankees.

Playing George, Jason Alexander originally drew on comedy inspirations that go back to his schoolyard days. "When I auditioned for the show in New York," he recalled during an appearance on *Live With Regis and Kathie Lee*, "it was just me and a camera. And I read a couple of pages from the pilot script. And I said, 'Boy, I need something. He kind of seems like a Woody Allen type of guy.' So I brought a pair of glasses. And they said, 'We like the glasses.' "

"If you go back and look at [George's] early episodes, you're seeing a guy do a really blatant Woody Allen imitation," Alexander once confessed.

Still, for all the bizarre situations that Woody Allen has written himself into, there was just no way of stretching the persona to cover some of the weirdness on *Seinfeld*. That is, until you bring in Larry David, *Seinfeld*'s cocreator, executive producer, and all-around guru.

"If there was something that I questioned, some behavior thing, I'd say, 'Nobody would do this,' " Alexander said. "And Larry would say, 'This happened to me, and this is what I did.' So instead of doing Woody Allen impressions, I started doing Larry David impressions."

Given the attention that George attracts, the show could have been called *George's World*. "George is Larry David's id," said Larry Charles. "He embodies all the dark impulses that Larry David has occasionally acted upon."

David, who bullied audiences that dared not to laugh at his stand-up routines, channels some of the worst human characteristics through George—including jealousy and rage—brought out by his crazy parents, his unemployment, or his disastrous dating history.

"In any other show my character would have cut his own throat by this point," Alexander said. "There are times when George walks the line of really being kind of hateful, but ultimately his heart's in the right place."

Lady Elaine

Elaine Benes may be the hardest character to write for. She's attractive, employed, and has a busy—if disappointing—love life. Yet the character has such a one-of-the-boys quality that the writers have found she can handle plot lines originally meant for George or Jerry. In fact, having bizarre circumstances surround the show's most normal character makes Elaine—striving for grace in ungraceful surroundings—even funnier. One would expect Jerry or George to fall into relationships that are doomed before they begin—but Elaine?

The show added Elaine after the pilot to ease pressure from the network to dress up the show with a beautiful woman. Although they wanted a permanent love interest for Jerry, the brass settled for a platonic ex-girlfriend, a move Larry and Jerry believed would give them more situations to put her in.

"We didn't want to get into a will they–won't they sex thing, so we figured an ex-girlfriend was a good way to get around that," Seinfeld said.

Comedian and *Seinfeld* writer Carol Leifer likes the way the show puts women into situations other sitcoms wouldn't. Like, for example, when Elaine invites her girlfriends over to play poker in "The Cigar Store Indian."

"[T]hat's what's great about the show," Leifer said. "I think on any other sitcom they'd make a big deal about it . . . Here, it's a given that a woman and her friends can play poker and it's not a big deal."

"She's one of the guys but hasn't forgotten she's a gal," summarizes Julia Louis-Dreyfus, the talented actress underneath Elaine's wall of hair. "Although most of the humor on the show is not gender-specific, she definitely gives a feminine sensibility, which is crucial."

When Elaine laments in "The Pool Guy" that she has no female friends left, Kramer puts it all into perspective: "You're a man's woman—you hate other women and they hate you."

"*Seinfeld* really is just a big boys club," adds Alexander, "and not the most emotionally mature set of boys to boot."

Elaine dated Jerry briefly, but, "There was a little problem with the physical chemistry," Jerry explained in the show's second episode ("The Stakeout"). They tried to resume a physical relationship—and even devised a set of ground rules in "The Deal," but broke up by the following episode, never again to mention their relationship in detail until "The Mango," where she reveals that she had "faked it" (or as Jerry says, committed "sexual perjury") every time the two slept together. A couple of seasons later, Elaine showed interest when he began making big bucks (enough to buy Morty a Cadillac). But by this time Jerry hardly noticed her advance.

Should Jerry and Elaine get back together?

"No," said Louis-Dreyfus. "That wouldn't be funny."

"My theory is that Jerry and Elaine will get married one day," she speculated in an interview, "but she'll be forty-eight and he'll be fiftysomething. Then they'll get divorced six months later." Or, Elaine could make good on her promise to Kramer—to marry him in fifty years if neither one is hitched by then. Then again, she could get on with her life.

"I think if she really had it together she would move on and get into a different social scene," Julia told *Dateline*. "But for some reason, she's held up."

"The reality is that these four characters are a pathetic group, and they should disassemble promptly," she explained. "I mean, if you stand back from it and look at what happens every week, they do terrible things to one another. And yet they continue to hang out. It's sociopathic. It's nuts! This is a sick group of people."

The fact that Elaine has so much going for her—especially compared to Jerry's other friends, George and Kramer—makes her part a tough one to write. "It didn't make sense that she was hanging out with these guys," said Larry Charles. "She's got a career, she's beautiful, she's friendly and funny and charming. We had to start exploring the darker sides of her personality—her compulsion to be honest—which would get her into trouble, her bad taste in men, a career that was stalled out and frustrating to her."

Elaine's penchant for calling it like it is has gotten her—and her friends—

As Elaine Benes, Julia Louis-Dreyfus has the rare ability to charm both male and female viewers with her humor and natural good looks. (Jeff Mayer/Star File)

into some of *Seinfeld*'s most memorable situations. In "The Pilot," Elaine rebuffs the advances of the NBC president, belittles his job, and admits she doesn't watch television, even though Jerry's TV deal hangs in the balance. She loses numerous boyfriends because she cannot accept minor flaws: he fails to use exclamation points, he shares a name with a serial killer, he dresses like a communist, or a podiatrist is not a "real doctor."

"I once broke up with someone for not offering me pie," is typical of Elaine's love life. Will she ever have a serious romance? Don't count on it.

"I hate men, but I'm not a lesbian," she told a stranger in "The Subway."

As for a relationship with Jerry, George, or Kramer, "that wouldn't be funny," Louis-Dreyfus told the *New York Times*. But, "I think under the right circumstances, at just the right moment, Elaine would sleep with any one of them."

Elaine is also a repository of interesting character details. She likes airline food, knows her Big Band music, and showed a lot of poise in her job as a menial personal assistant to Mr. Pitt—even though it meant shopping for his tube socks, sharpening pencils, and picking the salt off of pretzels. Her next job—as copy writer for the J. Peterman catalog—puts her in even more surreal situations, like having to write exotic stories about shoes and bras to impress her garrulous, globe-trotting boss. Elaine even inspired an entry in the real J. Peterman catalog, for a wool and silk sweater "very good for coffee shop chitchat, blind dates, neurotic friends."

The K-Man

Jerry once explained that Kramer "is the guy that is your friend by virtue of his proximity. There are a lot of people that are friends because they're nearby and it's nice to have somebody around."

Kramer, Jerry's next-door neighbor (and friend by default to George and

Elaine), is the wild one. He's the guy who gets rid of his refrigerator so he'll eat more fresh food, plans to build levels in his apartment in lieu of furniture, and covers his walls with fake wood wallpaper to get the feeling of a ski lodge. He can attract women with his jacket or merely his *kavorca* (Latvian for "the lure of the animal").

"These are my buddies," explained Michael Richards, the Emmy-winning actor who plays Kramer. "I know whenever I go into Jerry's apartment I'm going to get involved in something. And involvement means living."

Richards said slipping into the Kramer character is about as easy as slipping on a vintage Shirt-Jac.

"Kramer takes over when I put on the shoes and when I wear some of the clothing during rehearsal," he explained. "Kramer comes through. It's like channeling."

When the show started, people wrote that Michael was doing a Christopher Lloyd imitation, recalled costar Jason Alexander, referring to the Reverend Jim character on the acclaimed *Taxi*. "That had to hurt, because Michael would never copy anyone, and if anyone was doing an imitation, it was *me*. I shamelessly ripped off Woody Allen."

So what is it that makes Kramer funny?

"It's his sincerity, his commitment to a situation," Richards said. "And he's a fighter. We did a show where George was being real mousy. Kramer tells him to stand up."

After more than a hundred episodes, Richards says he keeps his character fresh by "finding comedy" in every scene. He created a small background for the character, "to justify the way he dresses and why he comes through the door the way he does. But I keep it to myself."

"If I come through the door, I've got to have a reason for coming in," he explained. "One show, I decided my sink had overflowed, even though it's not in the script. So I come into Jerry's apartment, unroll all his paper towels while saying my line. It's crazy. No one else knows why. But I got a big laugh. To find those moments fascinates me."

"I came up with this kind of entrance because I had to fit myself into the scene," he told *Dateline*. "And when I come in I gotta really come in."

Ironically, the zany one tends to be the group's etiquette watchdog. "Without rules, there's chaos," Kramer declares at one point. He's the one who chides Jerry for not offering the furniture moving men a drink. He also urges Jerry to make a morning-after thank-you call to a man who plied them with National Hockey League playoff tickets (albeit so he could get more tickets).

"Good manners are the glue of society," Kramer says in "The Face Painter." "If you don't want to be a part of society, Jerry, why don't you get in your car and move to the East Side!?!"

"I think what's so refreshing about Kramer is you don't know who his parents are," Richards explained in an early interview. "You don't know his apartment, you don't know what kind of car he drives, you don't know where he shops, you don't know what he eats. You don't know anything about the man. Yet, he's become so popular. There's a moment there where people can just go, 'Ah, I don't know anything.' That's what we love about the character. It's a show about nothing and we don't know anything about him."

Now, of course, we've seen his mother Babs (played to over-the-top perfection by veteran character-actress Sheree North), who revealed Kramer's first name. We've also seen his apartment, car, eating habits, and favorite stores. Yet Richards is still able to bring something fresh to the show.

Seinfeld Girlfriends: 15 Minutes of Fame

What's the shortest acting gig in TV history? For men, the record is probably held by the red-shirted security guards on *Star Trek*. For women, however, that honor belongs to the bevy of beauties playing Jerry's dates *du jour* on *Seinfeld*.

"The shortest lifespan for an actress is to be a guest star on the *Seinfeld* show," Jason Alexander said on NBC's *Dateline*. "You know you've got one episode and you're gone. Because relationships just do not work here." In fact, Jerry says, his TV counterpart will never get hitched because, "We enjoy casting the weekly girlfriend too much."

Despite his attempts to keep "the ugly side" hidden from girlfriends for at least six months (thus throwing off "the whole learning curve"), Jerry usually manages to screw up his relationships pretty quickly. Here are some of the actresses who survived the experience and went on to gainful employment:

• Jessica Lundy, who played the waitress Naomi in "The Watch" and "The Bubble Boy," created the laugh that sounded like "Elmer Fudd sitting on a juicer." She went on to star as Gloria Utz in NBC's *Hope and Gloria*.

• *Friends* star Courtney Cox (Monica) wanted to be more than friends with Jerry in her guest spot on *Seinfeld*. In "The Wife," she pretended to be Mrs. Meryl Seinfeld in order to use Jerry's dry cleaning discount. But the responsibility of the pretend marriage was too much for Jerry—and he started using his discount on another woman.

• Jane Leeves, who plays the English housekeeper Daphne on *Frasier*, portrayed the

The Others

Of course, some of the most popular characters only show up occasionally. When the writers need to bring in an outside element, they usually do it through the cast of supporting characters. Jerry's parents, Helen and Morty

As Sidra, spectacular Teri Hatcher found Jerry less than super in "The Implant." She became Lois Lane in ABC's *Lois & Clark: The New Adventures of Superman*. (© 1995 Capital Cities/ABC, Inc., Timothy White)

inexperienced Marla in "The Virgin" and "The Contest." Eventually she loses her virginity to an unseen John F. Kennedy Jr. in "The Pilot."

• Teri Hatcher, better known as Lois Lane on ABC's *Lois & Clark: The New Adventures of Superman*, made her mark in "The Implant" as the mysterious Sidra, whose "real and spectacular" breasts eluded Jerry's hands. Hatcher reprised her role at the end of "The Pilot," watching Jerry's ill-fated network debut with Sal Bass.

And let's not forget George's doomed relationships . . .

• George tried to impress Rosalind Allen (as Diane) in "The Marine Biologist" by pretending to be a marine biologist. Prophetic, perhaps, since she went on to play Dr. Wendy Smith on NBC's undersea drama, *seaQuest DSV*.

• Vicky Lewis, who played George's secretary, Ada, in "The Secretary" and "The Race," is now seen as Beth in NBC's *NewsRadio*.

Seinfeld (Liz Sheridan and Barney Martin), are a sure source of laughs for us and neuroses for Jerry. Estelle Harris and Jerry Stiller, as George's parents Estelle and Frank Costanza, with their constant bickering, steal almost every scene they're in.

Perhaps the most welcome (or unwelcome) character is Newman, the postal worker neighbor whom Jerry calls "pure evil." While he was originally conceived as a goofball pal of Kramer's and a nemesis of Jerry, Newman's role was expanded to become a wizened sage who settles a dispute over a bike ("The Seven") and a mafia hit man who masterminds a dognapping ("The Engagement").

"There is never a bad scene with Newman," said Peter Mehlman, "because Newman is brought in when he is *really* needed. Wayne Knight, who plays Newman, may be the greatest comedy machine in the world. This guy is just the scariest brilliant actor in the world. He is so funny. We go nuts for him."

"If our show is like *Abbott and Costello*, then [Newman] is the 'Stinky' of the show," said Larry Charles, referring to the irritating (but hilarious) child who lived next door to Bud and Lou in their short-lived but influential sitcom.

Writing About Nothing

Larry David has a rule for writing *Seinfeld* scripts: "No hugging, no learning."

"Our philosophy is, Ninety-nine percent of the world is on the verge of tears at any moment. What's the big deal to push them over?" writer-producer Peter Mehlman once told a writing seminar.

The only time the show came close to poignancy, according to Mehlman, was in 1991's "The Deal," in which Jerry and Elaine agree to sleep together but not get caught up in the usual relationship traps. The situation was never mentioned again, and the show never attempted to recreate that serious a moment.

It might have worked on *Cheers*, *The Mary Tyler Moore Show*, and *Taxi*, Mehlman conceded, but "it's not for us."

Writers must pitch their story ideas to Larry before they begin writing. As Mehlman told aspiring writers, each scene has to be inherently funny in its description. In the domain of *Seinfeld*, it is the situations, not the words, with which the audience must identify. "If it's the dialogue that's making the scene funny, then you're in trouble," Mehlman said.

Despite an influx of eleven writers in 1993, Seinfeld and David exert control over every line of every story. No matter who gets credit for the script, each episode is given a final combing over by the cocreators, who admit to doing drastic rewrites. "We were adamant about not doing a show where ten writers would sit around a table and a script would be written by committee," David said.

Each episode also has to be quirky, Seinfeld said. And if it can happen or has happened on TV—even forty years ago—according to Seinfeld, it's headed for the trash can.

And while *Seinfeld* has shown some of the most original plot devices in years, the show goes way beyond the single-gag concept of traditional sitcoms. The genius of the show—and Larry David—is tying everything together in the end. "Act Two," Seinfeld once said, "is what separates the men from the boys."

Larry David and Jerry Seinfeld also have a knack for injecting the characters' dialogue with sports jargon or other technical lingo.

However, the word play is not limited to catch phrases and situationally funny words, such as "master of your domain" (one who refrains from masturbating) and "Mulva" (Jerry's stab at guessing the name of a woman whose name rhymes with a female body part). "The real linguistic lure of *Seinfeld* [is] . . . the use of understatement and indirection, of not saying much of anything while making everything perfectly clear," noted James Gorman in the "On Language" column in *New York Times Magazine*. "It's really the opposite of the language of children—abstract, not concrete; all connotation, no denotation. A child can watch a racy *Seinfeld* episode and not understand a word—or rather understand every word but not have a clue as to what's going on."

While the show is often said to be about nothing (that idea came from the show itself, when Jerry and George pitched NBC their own show, *Jerry*, about nothing) it is actually about details, Seinfeld said. And, in fact, it was originally pitched as a show "about conversations," which perhaps turned out to be the most accurate description of all.

"We joke that it's about nothing because there's no concept behind the show, there's nothing intrinsically funny in the situation," Jerry explained in his *Playboy* interview. "It's just about four people. There's no thread. No high concept."

While it may indeed be about something, the show likes to have fun with its nothing reputation. In "The Phone Message," Jerry says he hates Dockers commercials because "they're talking about nothing!" In "The Airport," Jerry charms a supermodel aboard a plane who declares, "I never met a man who knew so much about nothing."

"We're amused," said Louis-Dreyfus. "It's clearly not about nothing. But also, it is about nothing, because ten minutes after you've seen it, you can't really remember what you saw."

If there is a theme, perhaps it is that a bad day can, in fact, get worse.

For the writers, life is "constantly looking for what's completely embarrassing to you and then looking for ways of getting out of it through scheming and then lying," said writer-producer Peter Mehlman. He describes the basic plot as "Boy meets girl. Boy loses girl. Boy almost gets girl back. Boy loses girl for good." Of course, the same formula can be—and is often—applied to Elaine.

Spy magazine even went so far as to create a cheeky "*Seinfeld*-O-Matic" chart to help aspiring writers create a *Seinfeld* script the way one might order a combination plate in a Chinese restaurant—one plot line from column A, one from column B, etc.

"You just give me a bowl of soup and there's thirty minutes," Seinfeld told *Entertainment Tonight*. "When you can make a show out of that, you're not going to run out of ideas."

A TV reporter asked Jerry why an episode like "The Parking Garage"—in which the characters spend the entire thirty minutes looking for their car—hits a nerve with viewers. "Because people have been in that situation before," he explained. "Taking it and making it into a whole show—that was the idea that no one ever did before."

"My theory is that Larry and Jerry are the Lennon-McCartney of comedy," said Carol Leifer. "When Larry did stand-up, the comedians would love it—he's more on the edge, more cerebral, more dark and brooding. And Jerry has more of a pop sensibility, such a good eye for conveying it to the masses. He's lighter and fluffier. He has that one-liner thing. He said that if he didn't go into show business, he probably would have gone into advertising. He would be good at that."

Although he once welcomed unsolicited scripts (and phoned struggling

Hot Wheels

A classic 1954 Porsche 536 Speedster owned by Jerry Seinfeld fetched $82,950 at a 1997 auction. The car, a shiny white beauty with a black leather interior, was purchased by the Yankee Candle Car Museum in South Deerfield, Mass. after a round of intense bidding. The car had a famous owner before Seinfeld—race car legend Dan Gurney. No word on how much "John" Voight's Chrysler LeBaron went for.

writers to offer comments), writer-producer Larry Charles said the phenomenon of ordinary people writing scripts became overwhelming. Once the tide swelled to thousands of scripts per month, they started going unopened into the garbage.

"It's absurd," he commented at the time. "Everyone thinks they understand the show. They think it's easy to write, which is the first mistake."

"Everybody says, 'This show is my life,'" explained Mehlman. "And they're right—this show is your life." Nevertheless, Mehlman said the writing staff never used a single plot line from a freelance script.

"People really think it is about nothing so you can write endless banter . . . That goes to nowhere," Mehlman said. "That 'show about nothing' thing is really deceptive, I think."

Seinfeld says the people who write these "spec" scripts and approach him on the street with ideas for the show "may be funny enough to get them through that moment at the water cooler, but they're not funny enough to be on television in front of millions of people and have them buy a Geo Prizm as a result."

While there has been some controversy over the show's use of sensitive subjects—Nazis, homophobia, the handicapped, the O.J. Simpson case, racism, date rape, abortion, and sexual politics—the politically incorrect topics tend to be overshadowed by the inherent humor of the situations.

"Even if we are being kind of offensive, the laughs are so strong that you don't taste anything else," explained Mehlman. "Laughter is a very strong spice."

Ironically, perhaps, the show won a GLAAD/LA Media Award from the Gay and Lesbian Alliance Against Defamation for its positive depiction of its homosexual characters. One episode cited was "The Outing," in which a newspaper reports that Jerry and George are lovers. The guys are very upset and attempt to convince everyone that they aren't gay, "not that there's anything wrong with that." The other episode cited, "The Smelly Car," finds George supportive of Susan, his one-time girlfriend and eventual fiancée, who had suddenly become a lesbian. In another episode, "The Opposite," Jerry even mentions one of homosexuality's big "selling points": "If you're going out with someone your size, you double your wardrobe."

And even though George frets over a physical reaction from a massage by a man—the humor is never mean-spirited.

"Certain subjects are a little more difficult to deal with than others," Seinfeld told NBC's *Dateline.* "And I don't shy away from something that might be hard to handle. Sometimes we succeed and sometimes we don't."

"The Contest," one of the most popular episodes and the highest-rated rerun, featured a competition to see which person could abstain from masturbation the longest. It was so skillfully done that neither NBC nor Castle Rock, both of which must sign off on every script, had any objections.

"I think the key thing is a state of utter honesty or reality," said Larry Charles. "It's not something you see very often on other sitcoms. We force the characters to face themselves and explore the darker sides of their personalities—to push the barriers on what they've done before."

"If I may be so immodest, it takes some pretty skillful writing to do these things and make them comfortable for people to watch on a mass level," Jerry explained. "Anybody can write a funny show about masturbation. But can you do it in an artful way that offends no one and, in fact, is even funnier than if you had come right out and talked about it? It takes skill."

"I really enjoy the art of euphemism," Seinfeld once explained, "especially compared to the shove-it-up-your-nose kind of stuff they usually do on TV."

Sometimes the show gets the same humorous effect by hitting to the opposite field—being blatant. While other shows might go their entire run without saying a word like *orgasm*, *Seinfeld* characters mention it thirteen times in twenty-two minutes in "The Mango."

Each episode's script takes about three or four days to get into its final form and a week to rehearse and shoot. In a medium where shows are produced months ahead of scheduled air times, the *Seinfeld* team is notorious for flying by the seat of its pants—which has worked in its favor since it can add last-minute bits of dialogue to reflect current events.

When it comes time to perform, the writers and actors have an understanding. As Jason Alexander once explained, "We don't write, they don't act." The writers, however, "write stuff that, on the page, doesn't seem like a joke, but they know we'll make it funny. That's a real tribute to us.

"All of us look out for one another," Alexander said. "We're there to help each other. If I think somebody's missing a beat, or if Jerry thinks I'm not saying a line in the rhythm it was written in or I could get a funnier read, we tell each other. We all share the ideas because we don't want the episode to be done and find out that it could have been better [but] somebody was afraid to open their mouth. Nobody's ego is such that we couldn't accept a great idea from somebody else. Nobody gets footnoted at the end of the show."

Julia agrees. "There's a certain sensibility that we all have about what's funny and we all share it," she said. "You know that doesn't happen a lot. In fact, I'll go so far as to say this is the last time it will happen.

"To tell you the truth, I think we find our show funnier than anybody else who watches," she confessed.

Bootleg "blooper" tapes show numerous examples of the cast cracking each other up—whether it be because of a blown line, a problem with a prop, or simply Kramer bounding through the door.

But one does not have to track down outtakes to find the cast smirking or holding back giggles. Louis-Dreyfus could barely make it through one of the final scenes of "The Junior Mint," in which a piece of candy apparently caused a miraculous medical recovery. "I couldn't get through a take of it," she recalled. "I think they had to cut around me. If you watch my back you can see it moving because I'm laughing so hard."

On the set, Jerry adds to the fun by spontaneously instituting "Jerry Challenges"—contests to see who can make the silliest voice or perform other ridiculous tasks.

After Tuesday-night filmings, the cast often goes out to a late dinner, where the competitions continue: they try to "out-order" each other to see who will come up with the most outlandish meals right before bedtime. Jason Alexander tells of "flooring" his castmates at one of the 1:00 A.M. dinners by ordering pastrami–roast beef club sandwiches and fries with gravy.

Is everything a competition? Jane Pauley once asked Seinfeld. It is, he said, "If you want to have fun."

Infiltrating NBC

NBC would like to forget that it initially passed on the *Seinfeld* project. If not for Rick Ludwin, NBC's senior vice president of specials, variety programs, and late night, the show might have wound up on cable, on Fox, or worse, in the vault.

"I have vivid memories of what they were saying," he told the *Los Angeles Times*. " 'It's too New York. It's too Jewish.' An executive who screened it in New York City actually asked, 'Does he have to be a comedian?' I'm not from New York, I'm not Jewish, and I thought it was funny, so I thought it could work."

So Ludwin convinced then-president of NBC Entertainment, Brandon Tartikoff, to let him take on the *Seinfeld* show. Ludwin then used money from the budget for specials, variety programs, and late-night shows to bankroll four new episodes which would run in May and June of 1990.

Despite a solid offer at the time to do twenty-four episodes for a cable network, *Seinfeld* stuck with Ludwin and NBC (and the four-episode offer) for a shot at network exposure. The gamble paid off. And Ludwin's division became responsible for *Seinfeld*—not the NBC prime-time department.

"That's why it came out not looking like it had been through the usual network big-production-company machine," Seinfeld said. "We kind of snuck in like the Trojan horse. We infiltrated this huge castle, undetected, and now we live there.

"It's a big reason for the success of the show," he explained. "Because we haven't been meddled with at all. They kept the originality of it intact. Even when they didn't like what we were doing or didn't understand it, they put it on the air."

Larry David, only half jokingly, said he would have liked to have gone on cable or the Fox network, however, because it would have been less pressure. "With my [stand-up] act, I liked to go on at one in the morning, when three-fourths of the audience had already gone," he explained. "There's no pressure. I like situations with no pressure."

Once the show made it to the air, it still had to find an audience—or have an audience find it. The show was juggled in the NBC schedule six times in four years. During which time it hovered in the ratings—too high to be considered a bomb, but too low to be considered a hit.

"They were actually trying to help," Jerry explained, "in their own networky way."

Luckily, the usual focus-group mentality was not used to judge the show, Seinfeld told the panel on Comedy Central's *Politically Incorrect*. "The focus groups, all the research, it's just crap," he said. "When we first did the pilot, every time they tested it people hated it. Every time they would test the audience they hated it. Men and women eighteen to forty-nine hated it. Forty-nine to sixty-three, zero to ten hated it. Everybody hated it. But we kept saying, 'But it's funny.' [NBC] put it on anyway because they thought it was funny."

The people who *were* watching, however, also thought it was funny. And they happened to be the right people to sell advertisers on the show: hip, urban, young, single. The same group that goes to the movies and restaurants and buys beer and cars.

"What made us develop was, despite being very low rated in the beginning, we had a very high demographic profile," Seinfeld explained. "Though we were technically bombing, the people watching were what they call advertiser desirable."

Things picked up in February 1993, when NBC shifted *Seinfeld* from Wednesdays at 9:00 P.M., where it took a beating against the more mainstream *Home Improvement*, to Thursdays at 9:30, in the plumb, post-*Cheers* slot. Immediately the show went from fortieth place to tenth, and soon after began topping new episodes of *Cheers*. Ever since, *Seinfeld* has placed consistently in the top ten, ratings-wise.

"To us, very quickly, it was a great show—the people making it were as excited about the show then as we are now," Seinfeld said. "And whether people caught on or not was something you just kind of watched and observed."

"In a weird way it took so long to happen," noted Louis-Dreyfus. "Here we shot sixty-something shows, and the first time I got a script, I thought 'My God, this is so good. Watch this take off.' Yet it didn't. It wasn't a huge flop, but it's taken a while for it to snowball."

In spring 1993, the show hit high stride, with audiences glued to Larry David's contiguous set of episodes involving Jerry and George's quest to pitch NBC their "show about nothing," concluding with a one-hour episode, "The Pilot," on the same night that *Cheers* said "last call" to its prime-time audience.

What a difference that year made. The following season opener, "The Mango," pulled a 19.3 rating (roughly 18 million households) and a 29 share (percent of televisions in use), up 54 percent over the previous year's premiere. The show would continue its upward push into the ratings until it was consistently in the top five.

While Jerry was gracious to the new converts, Larry's attitude was somewhat resentful. "As I've said before, if people didn't watch us on Wednesdays, I don't want them watching us on Thursdays," he griped to a reporter.

When *Cheers* left the air in 1993, NBC used *Seinfeld* as its Thursday-night anchor, a function it still has today. *Seinfeld* is credited with boosting *Frasier* (the *Cheers* spin-off, formerly on Thursday nights after *Seinfeld*) into the top ten. As a lead-in, *Seinfeld* even propelled the dreadful *Madman of the*

People into the top twenty (NBC canceled it anyway). *Friends*, which followed *Seinfeld* in 1994–95, had the double fortune of being a good show with a good lead-in and quickly attracted its own following.

The success of *Seinfeld* has made a cottage industry out of adult oriented, single-in-the-city sitcoms. The exception to the "singles" rule was NBC's *Mad About You*, with Paul Reiser as essentially a married Jerry Seinfeld. NBC created *Friends*, which got a "Seinfeldian" billing by the network as "A new comedy about . . . whatever." Most recently, NBC launched *Caroline in the City* and *The Single Guy* on Thursday night to attract the *Seinfeld/Friends* crowd. ABC's *Ellen* and Fox's *Living Single* are spun from similar threads.

President of NBC Entertainment, Warren Littlefield, says the show has become a drawing card for the *Seinfeld* network. "Talented people look at that and say, 'We want to be a part of that,' " explained Littlefield, who was himself parodied in several episodes. "It extends from on-camera talent to writers and producers who can assemble smart, funny adult comedies. *Seinfeld* really is the flagship for NBC."

It soon became apparent that *Seinfeld* was NBC's bread and butter, helping define the network as a purveyor of smart, savvy, sexy entertainment. The show became so powerful that it began calling the shots. Entertainment journalists confirm that NBC's powerful PR machine began cooling off to reporters when it came to *Seinfeld*, getting the go-ahead from Jerry Seinfeld before scheduling interviews. Few stars have wielded such power with their networks—perhaps Jackie Gleason, Lucille Ball, and Johnny Carson did, and now David Letterman does with CBS. In any case, *Seinfeld* was the tail wagging the NBC dog (or peacock). The network even bowed to the show when Larry David complained that promos were giving away too much of the plot.

The show aired its one hundredth episode in February 1995—a mile-

Timing Is Everything

Jerry Seinfeld has said time and again how he would like his show to go out a "gem." Below are two lists of classic TV shows. The only difference is that the first group went out "gems" while the latter group . . . well . . . didn't.

Five Shows That Went Out Ahead

The Honeymooners
  (1955–56)
Get Smart (1965–70)
Batman (1966–68)
The Odd Couple (1970–75)
Taxi (1978–83)

Five Shows That Ended Too Late

*All in the Family/Archie Bunker's
  Place* (1971–83)
*M*A*S*H* (1972–83)
Happy Days (1974–84)
Family Ties (1982–89)
Cheers (1982–93)

stone for any TV show, but especially for one whose creators never thought it would catch on. After a lull in the press, the landmark gave the media another excuse to write about Jerry and the gang. Even *Seinfeld* fan David Letterman commented on the hoopla. "One hundred episodes," Letterman said in a *Late Show* monologue. "That's fifty hours. Two full days of Jerry whining. Unbelievable!"

Despite the accolades, the show's creative team was concentrating more on the future than on the past, observed NBC's Littlefield: "The network is more focused on their achievement than they are—what it means, what it means for us."

Initially, the impact of reaching one hundred episodes was not lost on Jerry, who recalled wondering in the beginning: "How the hell are we going to do four of these things?"

"We've persevered," Jerry said of the characters in the introduction to his one hundredth show special, "because we're people—real TV people."

There were by then numerous signs that the show had become a part of American culture. In addition to the catch phrases ("shrinkage," "slip one past the goalie," "puffy shirt," "Soup Nazi," "Get *out!*") parroted throughout the day by fans, the show was having more lasting effects, inspiring everything from the coffee shop banter in Quentin Tarantino's film *Pulp Fiction* to a knock-off porno film, *Hindfeld*.

The question had become . . . how long can these TV people keep it up?

Adding fuel to the fire was the fact that *Seinfeld* was now syndicated in every major market in the country via a record 224 stations. Fans could watch the show five or six days a week. And with latter-day fans discovering the earlier (and, by some accounts, better) episodes, would they still enjoy the new ones?

In an interview in *Entertainment Weekly*, Jerry Seinfeld and Larry David tried to explain a backlash against the show. "There were a couple of articles where people tried to show that it was cool to hate it because everybody else liked it," Seinfeld said. "I can understand wanting to go against the grain on principle." Larry David chimed in, "Like if I was in high school and everybody was talking about this real popular guy, even if I liked him, I would start to hate him." Ironically, an article in that same issue of the magazine said *Seinfeld* had succumbed to "an entirely forgivable predictability" in the start of the 1993–94 season.

Seinfeld and David were both irritated by comments during the 1994–95 season that the show was "losing it." For that reason, Larry avoided the *Seinfeld* bulletin boards on the Internet, where new shows were picked apart and judged by fans minutes after their conclusion.

"It's absolutely ridiculous, these people," Seinfeld commented. "We're on top of every page of every episode. There's no way in the world that the show is slipping. It's just the nature of the cycle. People get used to it—they've seen Kramer, they've seen George and me. They just get used to it. If you went back to see *Schindler's List* every week for six months, you'd say, 'I think this movie is slipping.' "

"It doesn't matter what the people think," he told *TV Guide* in 1995. "They never say that about any other show, you know. Nobody ever talks about other shows slipping, because they were never anywhere to begin with. So when they say we're slipping, I take it as a backhanded compliment.

"As far as I'm concerned, the originality and the quality of the humor are up to par with everything we've ever done, if not better. But you cannot escape the sense of familiarity. That's why we have no intention of doing the show much longer."

Jason Alexander candidly admitted that he came into the 1995–96 season thinking "We're done. . . . I thought creatively we had sort of played it out," he confessed to *Entertainment Weekly*. "In the fifth and sixth seasons the show went in a different direction that I wasn't personally interested in. It went from being about the little things that happen to everybody, the minutiae of life, the funny examination of that stuff, to very broad story lines, very wacky."

And although the show received renewed appreciation from critics and fans in the season (due to episodes like "The Soup Nazi" and a continuous George-and-Susan storyline), it was time for Larry David to move on. In 1996, David made good on a promise to quit. A perfectionist who oversaw every bit of writing and production, David said in interviews he was feeling burned out and needed a break.

Before leaving, David penned the most controversial episode of all time, the 1995–96 season finale, "The Invitations," one of the darkest and most twisted comedies ever broadcast on network TV. In the show, George insists on buying the cheapest wedding invitations that he and Susan can find. But the envelopes, dutifully licked by Susan, contained toxic glue, causing her to keel over and die on screen. George, saved from his impending marriage and all its obligations and limitations, wastes little time before getting on the phone to ask out Marisa Tomei.

The episode divided fans, who were either floored by the intensity of David's black comedy or outraged that the series' sole likable character—one whose only flaw was her taste in men—was killed off so unceremoniously. The show also left viewers scratching their heads over Jerry's surprise engagement to a cynical, fast-talking cereal-eater named Jeannie, played by Janeane Garofalo. Despite the flood of angry phone calls fielded by NBC switchboards, the *Seinfeld* team got a good chuckle and one of its highest ratings ever.

David immediately got to work writing and casting his first major big-screen project, *Sour Grapes*. The movie, which marked David's film directorial debut as well, centered on two cousins who take a gambling vacation. One cousin borrows a quarter from the other and then hits the jackpot on a slot machine, causing all sorts of turmoil. Fears that David would lose his edge when he made the leap to the big screen were unwarranted. A test screening was considered so offensive by several editors of *Mademoiselle* that they walked out before the movie ended.

And *Seinfeld* went on, sans Larry David. It was still highly rated—the number-one sitcom and second overall behind *ER*—and was still being called the smartest and funniest show on television. But the world was left with the perennial question: "Will it be as good as it was in the old days?"

The Post-David Era

Jerry Seinfeld, now executive producer at the start of the 1996–97 season, was faced with a difficult problem. Should he attempt to continue in Larry David's style—or should he take the show into uncharted waters?

The *Seinfeld* formula already had been adopted by a dozen copycat shows. (Indeed, while pitching the "Jerry" sitcom to Japanese TV executives in "The Checks," George sums up the state of television affairs: "Every time you turn on a TV, all you see is four morons sitting around whining about their dates.") Jerry was smart enough to realize that even the best—and most original show—could benefit from some new ideas.

Starting with the season opener, "The Foundation," *Seinfeld* began to veer away from Larry David's dark brooding toward a lighter, fresher feel. *Seinfeld* became more ambitious, with bigger sets, more scenes, more music, more star power, and more advanced filming techniques. In "The Foundation," for example, a frustrated George looks upward and shouts "Khan!" in a complicated rotating camera shot that spoofed William Shatner in *Star Trek II: The Wrath of Khan*, Jerry and George's favorite *Star Trek* movie. (The same rotating camera effect would be used a year later, when a hungry and frustrated George looks skyward and screams "Twix!")

The single funniest shot, however, comes in "The Pothole," where Jerry is filmed from a toilet-eye view as he retrieves his girlfriend's toothbrush from the water of her commode.

Because of the longer, more intricate storylines and the demands on Jerry's time as top banana, he made the decision to altogether eliminate the opening comedy monologues, which had already been decreasing in frequency. With more time for the story, Jerry and his writers—who, as *Seinfeld* scribes, had reached the top of their profession—could spin their increasingly complex yarns.

Unchecked by David, Jerry was also free to develop stories, jokes, and sight gags that appealed to his cartoonish side. In "The Soul Mate," Jerry chases Newman through the halls of their apartment building in a scene— in fast motion with generic suspense music—that would not have been out of place in a *Scooby-Doo* episode. That same season's "The Little Jerry" concludes with a slow-motion spoof of old Hollywood boxing pictures— only this time the crowds are cheering for roosters in a cockfight.

Music plays a role in the newer episodes. Sheena Easton's hit "Nine to Five (Morning Train)" is used in two montages: one showing Kramer at work in the investment world ("The Bizarro Jerry"); the other showing a "handicapped" George going through his day at the Play Now playground equipment company ("The Butter Shave"). And while Jerry does some soul-searching to choose between his girlfriend or the silly voice he assigns to her belly button (in "The Voice"), we hear Lionel Richie's hit "Hello." In "The Checks" Elaine dates a guy who gets emotional whenever he hears the song "Desperado." There's even a bit of existentialism introduced, as Jerry and Kramer seem to switch bodies in "The Chicken Roaster," and Kramer takes on the characteristics of a dog in "The Andrea Doria."

Parade of Characters

Besides the complicated stories, ambitious productions, and music, Jerry also brought in guest stars (either as themselves or as new characters) to give the show some celebrity cachet. Obscure characters from earlier episodes made unexpected returns, while minor characters became more entwined in the *Seinfeld* gang's everyday lives.

Guest stars who appeared as themselves (a trail blazed in earlier seasons by such notables as Jon Voight and Bette Midler in "The Mom and Pop Store" and "The Understudy," respectively) included Alex Trebek, David Letterman, Yankees Bernie Williams and Derek Jeter (all in "The Abstinence"), Raquel Welch ("The Summer of George"), and the animal expert and talk-show staple Jim Fowler ("The Merv Griffin Show").

Other stars clamored for and got career-boosting character roles. Jill St. John and Robert Wagner played wedding guests in "The Yada Yada." Lloyd Bridges appeared as Izzy Mandelbaum ("The English Patient," "The Blood"). Gordon Jump caught on to George's handicap scheme as Play Now boss Mr. Thomassoulo ("The Voice"). Wilford Brimley played the stern postmaster general ("The Junk Mail"). *Melrose Place* villainess Marcia Cross became a life-saving dermatologist ("The Slicer"), and James Spader became a "rage-a-holic" in addition to an alcoholic ("The Apology").

In the first episode without David, "The Foundation," fans were delighted to revisit Dolores, a.k.a. Mulva (Susan Walters). And Carol (Lisa Mende), the Long Islander who urged Elaine, Kramer, and Jerry to "see the bay-bay" in "The Hamptons" returned, this time encouraging Elaine to *have* a "bay-bay" ("The Soul Mate").

In the next two years, the parade of recurring characters would include

Elaine's boss, catalog king J. Peterman (John O'Hurley); Elaine's on-again-off-again boyfriend, David Puddy (Patrick Warburton); George's Yankee boss Mr. Wilhelm (Richard Herd); Susan Ross's rich, WASP-y parents (Warren Frost and Grace Zabriskie); fast-talking lawyer Jackie Chiles (Phil Morris); Elaine's braless rival Sue Ellen Mischke (Brenda Strong); Jerry's nemesis, the annoying comic Kenny Bania (Steve Hytner); Elaine's former boss, Mr. Lippman (Richard Fancy); Rabbi Glickman (Bruce Mahler); George's rival, Lloyd Braun (Matt McCoy); perverted dentist Tim Whatley (Bryan Cranston); Jerry's annoying agent, Katie (Debra Jo Rupp); and, briefly, Jeannie (Janeane Garofalo), who ended the cliffhanger by mutually ending the engagement with Jerry.

Seinfeld even brought back two noncharacters in its final seasons: George pretended to sell computers to a "Mr. Vandelay" in "The Serenity Now," and pretends to be looking for a "Mr. Vandelay" in an effort to break the ice with a pretty office receptionist in "The Bizarro Jerry." And Kramer became "Dr. Van Nostrand" twice: once pretending to be a "Juilliard-trained dermatologist" ("The Slicer") and once pretending to be Elaine's doctor in a failed attempt to steal her medical records ("The Package").

Of course, fans of Newman and the Seinfeld and Costanza parents were not to be disappointed, as these characters continued to have many appearances.

Staying Unpredictable

Week after week, it became apparent that Jerry was throwing in little surprises to keep the show from seeming stale. The show's ninth season began with a shock—Jerry and George sporting mustaches (Kramer too)—that kept the audience wondering what would happen next.

With ratings and revenues higher than ever, *Seinfeld's* creative team could afford to think outside the box—and outside Jerry's apartment. The show's technical staff could create any environment dreamed up by the writers. In "The Bizarro Jerry," for example, the show's set decorators built a detailed apartment that was the exact opposite of Jerry's, complete with locking door, unicycle on the wall, and miniature statue of Bizarro in the background.

One of the most ambitious episodes ever was "The Betrayal" in late 1997, billed as the "all-backward episode" and inspired by the Harold Pinter play *Betrayal*, which starts at the end and finishes with the first scene. The *Seinfeld* episode begins with the ending credits and the gang arguing in the coffee shop. As the episode unfolds, scene by scene, in reverse order, we discover that the characters have come back from a wedding in India. We see not only the wedding but also the days and events leading up to it. The show was expensive to produce, requiring all new India sets and live elephants on the stage. Even the theme music was rerecorded using sitars and other traditional Indian instruments. Nevertheless, the comedy was never once in danger of being overshadowed by the sets.

The episode flashes back two years to a time when Elaine was dating the groom (fittingly named Pinter) and Jerry is learning about a new technological application called e-mail. In a wonderful surprise, even Susan is resurrected to add authenticity. Also explained, at the end—err, beginning—of the episode is the origin of a rift between Kramer and F.D.R. (Franklin Delano Romanowski) that involves a snowball. In another brilliant (and revealing) flashback, this time eleven years earlier, Jerry meets a non-imposing Kramer for the first time and makes the mistake of offering him some pizza and saying "We're neighbors. What's mine is yours."

Top 10 Scenes From *Seinfeld* in the Post–Larry David Era

- Elaine is trapped between Jerry, George, and Kramer on one side and their "bizzaro" counterparts on the other. ("The Bizarro Jerry")

- Jerry, dressed as a boxing coach, spars with a rooster, Little Jerry Seinfeld, before a cockfight. ("The Little Jerry")

- Elaine dances at a company party—and it is described by George as "a full-body dry heave set to music." (The Little Kicks")

- George poses in his underwear while Kramer conducts what is supposed to be a sexy fashion shoot." (The Package")

- Kramer puts his three Japanese visitors to bed—in an oversized chest of drawers. ("The Checks")

- In a page borrowed from the film *Apocalypse Now,* Elaine finds Peterman in Burma, only to learn he has become an insane "white poet warlord." (The Chicken Roaster")

- George brings his co-op board to tears by describing the incidents that made up his pathetic life. ("The Andrea Doria")

- A gang of senior citizen bikers engage George in a low-speed motorized scooter chase. ("The Voice")

- Kramer rebuilds the old *Merv Griffin Show* set in his apartment, then conducts all of his conversations as if they were talk-show interviews. ("The Merv Griffin Show")

- Kramer washes his dishes, cooks, and makes telephone calls all from the comfort of his shower. ("The Apology")

All of these innovations in the post-David era did not replace what *Seinfeld* fans had come to love—the nuances, the language, the minutiae—but merely added to them. The show still managed to come up with popular catchphrases in its final two seasons, most notably Frank Costanza's "serenity now!" mantra and the now-ubiquitous "yada, yada."

While the latter-day episodes continued to win bigger and bigger audi-

A Difficult Patient

Doctors diagnosed a 62-year-old Massachusetts man with *"Seinfeld* syncope" after he passed out three times from laughing at George Costanza's antics on TV. According to an article in a 1997 issue of *Catheterization and Cardiovascular Diagnosis*, the man laughed so hard in one instance that "he fell face first into his evening meal and was rescued by his wife." The real cause, according to the man's doctors, was that blood flow to the man's brain was diminished by blockages in several arteries—the result of smoking and high cholesterol levels. When the man was calm, plenty of blood reached his brain. But when he laughed hysterically—usually during a Costanza screw-up—pressure in his chest pushed down on his heart, reducing blood flow. Doctors were able to treat the condition—and more importantly—they gave him the green light to watch *Seinfeld* again.

ences, they met with some resistance from a large number of long-time fans and a handful of TV critics, who felt that the show's original appeal—flawed, identifiable characters caught in recognizable everyday situations—had been abandoned in favor of a contrived, buffoonish approach.

It should be noted, though, that many newcomer fans actually prefer the most recent episodes and find the earlier season's hard to grasp. Most fans, however, accepted the show's evolution, not unlike Beatles fans who stayed with the fab four after the simple, melodious early days of "Love Me Do" through their challenging, multi-layered tracks on *Sgt. Pepper* and *Abbey Road* albums.

And lest anyone think the characters got nicer without Larry David's influence, one need only recall that George made fun of an Andrea Doria survivor in a bid to get a larger apartment; created a bogus charity and made donations in coworkers' names in lieu of getting them Christmas presents; and drove a recovering alcoholic to the rum raisin ice cream. Elaine intentionally infected a coworker with her germs; Kramer got Jerry mixed up in mail fraud. And finally, Jerry told his Uncle Leo to open a package that he knew might contain a bomb.

Money Squabbles

Although Jerry Seinfeld had toyed with the idea of wrapping up the show after the 1996–97 season, it was his costars who nearly made that decision instead. Jason Alexander, Julia Louis-Dreyfus, and Michael Richards—the most popular comedy ensemble of the 1990s—decided they needed a raise. As actors—not creators, producers, or writers of the show—the trio were largely cut out of the huge profits made when *Seinfeld* went into syndication all over the world.

They were making an estimated $150,000 per episode—no paltry sum, but relatively small potatoes compared with the revenue Jerry would stand to make over the years in rerun rights. Even with standard residuals—monies paid each time an episode airs—they clearly would not be the prime benefactors from the work and the laughs they created. In early 1997, the trio banded together and demanded $1 million per episode for the upcoming season in order to make up for the syndicated revenue they would never see. The trio was said to be particularly upset that they were making less than Jerry's managers, who were attached to the show as coexecutive producers.

By comparison, Jerry was making $500,000 per episode, and as a creator and part owner of the show, he had earned about $45 million from the $3

Tie-ing One on for Charity

Jerry Seinfeld, comedian . . . and fashion designer? The Sein donated a drawing to Save The Children, one of the world's largest charities, to be used as a necktie design. A portion of the proceeds from the sale of the tie was used to benefit children in the U.S. and abroad. Other celebs participating included Whoopi Goldberg, Larry King, Tom Chapin, and the cast of *Friends*.

million per episode generated by syndication rights. In 1997, Jerry Seinfeld was ranked the sixth wealthiest entertainer by *Forbes* magazine, with gross income of $94 million, including his salary from *Seinfeld* and his American Express commercials. The only personalities ahead of him were, in descending order, Steven Spielberg, George Lucas, Oprah Winfrey, Michael Crichton, and the Beatles.

NBC, hesitant to set a salary precedent for its stars, refused to go above $250,000 each per episode and was reportedly considering giving the three actors stock options for General Electric, the network's parent company.

As the stalemate dragged on, the actors stood firm. "I was worried that people were going to look at us as nothing more than a bunch of greedy pigs who were trying to hold everybody up and didn't care whether the show came back or not," Michael Richards said in a *TV Guide* interview. "And that wasn't the case at all. It's just that, in view of how successful the show has become, we needed to be a part of that. It's the same with sports salaries. You see these great players making so much money and go, 'How can they be worth that?'

Then when you start to think of what these teams generate in revenue, you begin to understand. Well, we're the Chicago Bulls of television."

After months of wrangling, NBC and the stars reached an agreement— a two-season deal worth about $13 million a year ($600,000 per episode) for each of the three actors. NBC counted on making the money back in advertising revenue.

But what worried NBC (as well as other networks) was how the settlement would affect other sitcom stars. And in fact, following the agreement with the *Seinfeld* stars, other sitcom luminaries demanded raises of their own. Even Wayne "Newman" Knight got a raise, to about $60,000 per appearance on *Seinfeld*. Elsewhere, the talented Knight, hot off a starring role opposite Michael Jordan in the 1996 film *Space Jam*, signed a $2 million, three-year contract with the producers of NBC hit *3rd Rock From the Sun* to make sure he continued to wear a different uniform, that of Officer Don, the lawman love interest to sexy alien Sally (Kristen Johnston).

Out With a Bang

Ironically, the *Seinfeld* players would not see the two seasons they had been contracted to do. In November 1997, Jerry was again unsure about whether to keep the show going. He told *New York Times* TV writer Bill Carter that he would make up his mind about continuing the show in about a month's time. "I'm feeling very good," Seinfeld said. "I don't mean to be cagey. But I just don't know what I'm going to do yet."

Seinfeld: Good for the Big Apple?

In an editorial, the *New York Post* praised *Seinfeld* for changing perceptions about New York City. Whereas the town had previously been depicted as dangerous, violent, and dirty, the show portrayed it as a place where anything—even good things—could happen. Kramer could meet Bette Midler in Central Park; Elaine could go from being a menial personal assistant to being a catalog maven; and George could fulfill his dream of working for the Yankees. Jerry, a standup comic, could date the most beautiful women in the world, one after another.

"*Seinfeld* brought a knowing, ironic, self-mocking post-modern glamour to a city desperately in need of it," the *Post* said. "The show's success inspired a million set-in–New York sitcoms, but only *Seinfeld* has made the city into a character as vivid and amusing as the rest of the cast. And for reminding America, and New York itself, of the eccentricities and quirks that help make this city great, *Seinfeld* has our thanks."

Responding to a newspaper poll that found audiences divided over whether the show was holding up comedically, Jerry cited a 1 percent increase in ratings on NBC and higher viewership for the syndicated shows. "If the ratings were down, I might think they had a point, but we're growing," he told Carter. "To be still growing after all these years on the air is just astounding. Any critical comment is just an individual opinion.

"I come out of the world of stand-up comedy. If you're in front of a house of five thousand and two people aren't laughing, believe me, that's no problem. We have thirty million people watching every week."

In that interview, Seinfeld lamented that there was no entertainer who had ever been in his situation whom he could ask for help. "I thought about calling Bill Cosby or Mary Tyler Moore. But there's no show that's been in this position so late in its run," he said. As Carter, a veteran industry reporter, pointed out, *The Cosby Show* was number 16 in its final season and *The Mary Tyler Moore Show* was out of the top 25 in its seventh and last season. However, he noted that *The Andy Griffith Show* did end its eighth and final season in the number 1 position.

"It is important for me to go out in full blazing color," Seinfeld said. "Most shows don't time it right. They hang on too long. If people are not terribly upset when we go off I will have judged it wrong." True to his word, Seinfeld announced Christmas Day 1997 that the show would cease production after its current season.

The decision immediately grabbed headlines. The *New York Times* rushed the story onto its Website that night. The following day it ran in the noteworthy upper-left corner of page one—the above-the-fold slot people see first when picking up the paper. Wire services, TV broadcasts, and other newspapers scrambled to include the news that the *Times*—and Carter—had broken.

Seinfeld fans responded instantly to the reports on the Internet. Most agreed with Jerry that the show should go out while it was at its peak rather than have the star "turn off the engines and glide for maybe two years," as he had said in the article.

Around New York, news crews gathered outside notable *Seinfeld* fan haunts—the Upper West Side restaurant that doubles as the Monk's Diner facade and the "strict" soup man's shop—to get reactions to the news. While

Will the Real Peterman Please Stand Up?

Anyone familiar with the J. Peterman catalog knows the company takes a few liberties with celebrity names. There's the cap that Hemingway *might've worn* or the blazer that David Niven made famous. But when a *Seinfeld* character named Mr. Peterman appeared out of nowhere and gave Elaine a job at his catalog, the tables were turned.

"I knew nothing about it," the real John Peterman said at a rare public appearance this year. "They didn't call, they didn't ask. They just did it."

"I was on the red-eye from California to Lexington," Peterman explained. "I arrived on a Friday morning, went to the office, and they said, 'You were on *Seinfeld* last night.' I said, 'No, I was on an airplane.' They said, 'No, you were on *Seinfeld!*' So I said, 'What's *Seinfeld?*' because—cross my heart—I had never watched it."

Since he consoled a desperate Elaine in the 1994–95 season finale "The Understudy," Mr. Peterman (played to staccato soap-opera perfection by John O'Hurley) has accused Elaine of being an opium fiend; blamed George for the death of his mother; marketed a line of bras as ladies' tops; bought J.F.K.'s golf clubs; and tried to foster a romance between Elaine and a hearing-impaired employee before he himself suffered a nervous breakdown and fled to Burma. Apparently a cartoon aficionado, Peterman was also the one who realized that Elaine's *New Yorker* cartoon was actually a subconscious rip-off of an old Ziggy strip.

Being a character on *Seinfeld* has its "plusses and minuses," Peterman said. "The plusses: 37 million people hear the name." The minus is that the Mr. Peterman character is, as he puts it, "an asshole."

There are other differences between the catalog founder and his TV counterpart. The real Peterman lives and works in Lexington, Kentucky, not New York City. He also did not get his start in the Peace Corps clothing the Pygmies. After college, the real Peterman played minor league baseball in the Pirates organization, before moving on to several jobs in sales and marketing. In fall 1988 he launched his first catalog, with only seven items. Today, the catalog is filled with unique, stylish items designed to bring a sense of romance and adventure to the lives of Peterman customers.

Though it's exaggerated on *Seinfeld*, the J. Peterman catalog does in fact feature rambling product descriptions that appeal to customers' intelligence and sense of humor. References to *Seinfeld* have crept into the catalog more than once. Consider this description for the Wool and Silk Pullover: "I found her in the rain. No umbrella. Disheveled. Crying. Something about Korean beauticians? But very stylish (wearing one of our coats). I offered her a job writing for the catalogue. That cheered her up. . . . This sweater? Tunic length. Very good for coffee shop chitchat, blind dates, neurotic friends."

The real J. Peterman catalog can be a fun read. To request a copy, call (800) 231-7341. Overseas call (606) 254-5444 or surf to http://www.jpeterman.com.

The real J. Peterman. (Van Nostrand Archive)

Return to Sender

In yet another case of life imitating *Seinfeld* art, two New Yorkers were caught trucking thousands of empty soda bottles and cans to Detroit in 1997 in order to redeem them for the 10-cent deposit. The 10-cent deposit, which is double the five-cent deposit found in most every other state, originally lured Kramer and Newman to attempt a similar run in 1996's one-hour episode, "The Bottle Deposit." The real-life knuckleheads were arraigned in Detroit on felony counts of false pretenses over $100.

the reruns will undoubtedly play for years—indeed decades—to come, the thought of Thursdays without new installments of *Seinfeld* was, for many, a tough pill to swallow.

In a brief statement, NBC said, "To keep a show of this caliber at its peak has been a great undertaking. We respect Jerry's decision that at the end of this season it's time to move on."

Publicly, NBC officials said they would not try to get Jerry to change his mind, but a variety of sources reported that Jerry had been offered as much as $5 million per episode to keep the show alive one more year. "They did everything humanly possible," Seinfeld told the *New York Times*. "But money was not a factor at all. I was not even looking for a raise. We've all seen a million athletes where you say, 'I wish they didn't do those last two years.' For me, this is all about timing. My life is all about timing. As a comedian, my sense of timing is everything."

Several days before the announcement was made, Jerry Seinfeld gathered his costars in his dressing room and told them of his decision. "It was pretty heavy, pretty wild," recalled Julia Louis-Dreyfus, in a *Time* magazine cover story (January 12, 1998). "There were no tears shed, but there was a lot of heart thumping." Of the meeting, Jerry said, "They just started making good money last year, but they were generous enough to respect the timing of the curve—not that they could have talked me out of it, I don't think."

As the final weeks of *Seinfeld* rolled on, the show continued to garner higher and higher ratings, as if viewers were gathering to see old friends off on a long vacation. Parties were planned around the country and around the world—for fans to get together May 21, 1998, and say good-bye to their favorite show.

Media watchers expected the finale to be the highest rated non–Super Bowl telecast in history. Executives were even hoping to beat the 60.3 rating and 77 share obtained by the final episode of *M*A*S*H* in the halcyon days before cable TV.

For NBC, it was clear the goose was about to stop laying golden eggs. NBC is said to have made about $200 million per season of *Seinfeld*, even after the paychecks cleared. For the network, the finale was a last chance to milk *Seinfeld's* advertisers for all they could. Rates for a 30-second spot were in the $2 million range.

The Future

No one knows what the future holds for the talented stars of *Seinfeld*—but it sure looks bright.

Jason Alexander is developing a stage-musical version of the 1955 film *Marty*. He plans to play the same role that earned an Oscar for Ernest Borgnine, and he said he hopes to bring the show to Broadway "the sooner the better." Having vowed to "retire" the George-type persona for at least two years after *Seinfeld* ceases production, Alexander has gone out of his way to showcase the full range of his performing talent in a variety of recent projects. He was part of a star-studded cast in the critically acclaimed 1997 ABC remake of *Cinderella* and costarred that year in a concert staging of the 1968 Burt Bacarach, Hal David, and Neil Simon musical *Promises, Promises* in

Newsworthy Polls

Ten percent of respondents to a *TV Guide* poll about TV and religion said they would like to discuss God with Jerry Seinfeld. Six percent said they would like the comic to be their child's Sunday school teacher.

One Labor Day weekend, Sprint asked TV watchers who is the most unproductive employee on television. The dubious honor went to beer-guzzling Norm Peterson of *Cheers* (37 percent), who was often unemployed; Homer Simpson of *The Simpsons* was next with 31 percent; followed by George Costanza (23 percent); and Mimi Bobeck, the makeup-laden scene stealer of *The Drew Carey Show*, with 9 percent of the vote.

Los Angeles. In 1996, he sang with the Boston Pops and toured several cities, bringing down the house with local orchestras. On the big screen, he won critical acclaim for his work in the bittersweet drama *Love! Valour! Compassion!*, taking on the role made famous by Nathan Lane when the show was staged on Broadway.

Julia Louis-Dreyfus, who returned to movies in Woody Allen's *Deconstructing Harry* (1997), has said she is eager to work with her husband, writer-producer Brad Hall.

Michael Richards, whose Kramer persona has been called the tip of the iceberg of his comic talent, has been inundated with feature film offers. Should he continue his movie career, the time away from *Seinfeld* will afford this methodical practitioner of the acting craft the luxury of time to work in a more relaxed atmosphere.

Some pundits speculated whether or not there would be a spin-off featuring George, Elaine, Kramer, Newman—or even the two sets of parents.

Any spin-off would have to be approved by Jerry Seinfeld and Larry David. But it is doubtful that the supporting players—among the most talented and multifaceted in the industry—would want to be nailed down to their *Seinfeld* characters.

As for Jerry, he's said he plans to go back to New York to write new material, reclaim his stand-up comedy spotlight, and catch up on all he has missed while doing the show. "I don't like the idea of doing movies," Jerry told interviewer Cindy Crawford on the talk show *Later*. "They take too long. If you go to a bad movie, it's two hours. If you're in a bad movie, it's two years. I just can't wait that long, just to say, 'That was awful.'"

Seinfeld told Crawford he feels no pressure to top himself, simply because: "I can't do it."

The Envelope, Please

Although *Seinfeld*'s cast and creators have become familiar faces at many of the entertainment industry's top awards shows, it's obvious Jerry Seinfeld doesn't get too carried away by these events.

As an Emmy presenter in 1994, Jerry did a routine about how the television industry expresses "how much we love our own work—a chance to say, 'Congratulations to us on another year's job well done.'

"Oh sure, most of us that are nominated tonight employ a phalanx of agents, managers, and publicists to tell us these things on a daily basis anyway," he quipped, "but you'd be surprised how much we enjoy hearing it just one more time on national television with millions of people watching. . . . [Tonight] is one night when our entire wonderful TV industry can gather to say, 'We like us. We *really* like us.' "

Upon receiving a Golden Globe Award for Best Actor, he looked around the auditorium and made the Freudian observation: "Wow, there's a lot of cleavage in this room!"

When Dick Clark asked about the "show about nothing" winning the Golden Globe Award for Best TV Series—Comedy/Musical, Jerry replied, "Awards are basically for nothing, so when you do a show about nothing, it's a natural."

When they're not winning awards, the cast is livening up these seemingly interminable ceremonies. In 1994 Jason Alexander paid tribute to the great theme songs of yesteryear with a tongue-in-cheek stab at the dreaded overblown production number at that year's Emmy Awards. In just a few minutes, Alexander saluted more than thirty theme songs—everything from *The Patty Duke Show* to *Cheers*, and even got a big kiss from Maureen McCormick during his rendition of *The Brady Bunch* theme. (Alexander was so popular he was brought back as cohost the following year.)

On the same program, Michael Richards floored the audience with his twitchy, nervous, speechless acceptance of the Emmy for Outstanding Supporting Actor in a Comedy Series—his second in two years. When he returned later to present an award, Richards was disheveled, with a rip across one knee and one foot bare. While the audience giggled in anticipation of an explanation, Richards deadpanned the presentation, then announced that the winner, who was not present, had been arrested in Tennessee.

Although he was among the top vote-getters in a 1994 poll to see who should host the Oscars, Jerry insisted he was not interested in that job. "I

Jerry adds one more to the show's trophy case. This time, it's the Emmy for Outstanding Comedy Series. (Vinnie Zuffante/Star File)

would not host an awards show," he told the American Comedy Awards audience in 1995. "I do not know why anyone would host an awards show. No matter how unbelievably well you do at it, the only thing that can happen is you get asked again to host an awards show."

When Jerry Seinfeld was left out of the 1997 Emmy nominations for Best Actor in A Comedy Series, he used his time as a presenter to give the voters a light scolding. Seinfeld, whose customary place among the nominees went to *Spin City*'s Michael J. Fox, told the audience, "I am a big fan of Michael J. Fox. I am a big fan of *Spin City*. He plays the mayor, or something. I, on the other hand, play myself. And I guess last year you people didn't quite buy me as me. I'll admit, I didn't quite feel myself last season."

Jerry took the omission in stride. "I really don't care," he told an interviewer. "We've won everything—all the Emmys. We've been very lucky."

In the U.S., *Seinfeld*, its cast, and its creators have won more than 50 major television awards, and been nominated for an astounding 200, a reflection of the high esteem the show holds among the voters—everyone from fellow writers and directors to fans and TV critics.

Even the nominees who didn't win are worth noting. Larry Thomas was nominated for an Emmy for his memorable guest appearance as the title character of "The Soup Nazi." Judge Reinhold was nominated for an Emmy for his portrayal of Elaine's close-talking boyfriend, Aaron, in "The Raincoats." Marlee Matlin was also noticed by the Emmy voters for her guest spot as Laura in "The Lip Reader." Jerry Stiller has racked up an Emmy nomination and an American Comedy Award nomination for his portrayal of George's easily outraged father.

Stand-up comic Janeane Garofalo, a favorite character on HBO's *The Larry Sanders Show*, received an American Comedy Award nomination for her work in "The Invitations."

In addition to his many acting nominations, Jason Alexander was nominated in 1993 for a Director's Guild award for his turn at the helm of the 1992 episode, "The Good Samaritan."

And the Winner Is . . .

Seinfeld

American Television Award, Best Situation Comedy Series, 1993

Emmy Award, Outstanding Comedy Series, 1993

Gay and Lesbian Alliance Against Defamation/Los Angeles Media Award, Outstanding Television Comedy Series, 1992, 1994

Golden Globe Award, Best TV Series—Comedy/Musical, 1994

Peabody Award, Best Television Entertainment, 1993

People's Choice Award, Favorite Television Comedy Series, 1994, 1996, 1997, 1998

Screen Actors Guild Award, Best Comedy, 1995

Television Critics Association Award, Outstanding Achievement in Comedy, 1992, 1993

Jerry Seinfeld

American Comedy Award, Funniest Male Performer in a Comedy Series, 1992, 1993

American Television Award, Best Lead Actor in a Situation Comedy Series, 1993

Golden Globe Award, Best Performance by an Actor in a TV Series—Comedy/Musical, 1994

People's Choice Award, Favorite Male TV Performer, 1995

Viewers for Quality Television Award, Best Actor in a Comedy Series, 1993

Jason Alexander

American Comedy Award, Funniest Supporting Male Performer in a Comedy Series, 1992, 1993

American Television Award, Best Supporting Actor in a Situation Comedy Series, 1993

Screen Actors Guild Award, Outstanding Performance by a Male Actor in a Comedy Series, 1994, 1995

Julia Louis-Dreyfus

American Comedy Award, Funniest Supporting Female Performer in a Comedy Series, 1993, 1994, 1995, 1997

American Television Award, Best Supporting Actress in a Situation Comedy, 1993

Emmy Award, Outstanding Supporting Actress in a Comedy Series, 1996

Golden Globe Award, Best Performance by an Actress in a Supporting Role in a Series, Miniseries or Motion Picture Made for Television, 1994

Screen Actors Guild Award, Outstanding Performance by a Female Actor in a Comedy Series, 1997

Viewers for Quality Television Award, Best Supporting Actress in a Comedy Series, 1992, 1993, 1994, 1997

Michael Richards

Emmy Award, Outstanding Supporting Actor in a Comedy Series, 1993, 1994, 1997

Jerry Seinfeld, Jason Alexander, Julia Louis-Dreyfus, and Michael Richards

Screen Actors Guild Award, Outstanding Ensemble Performance in a Comedy Series, 1994, 1995, 1997

Jerry Seinfeld/Larry David

Producers Guild of America/American Airlines Nova Award: Best Television Comedy Series, 1994

Larry David

Emmy Award, Outstanding Individual Achievement in Writing in a Comedy Series ("The Contest"), 1993

Writers Guild of America Award, Best Episodic Comedy ("The Contest"), 1994

Larry David/Lawrence H. Levy

Writers Guild of America Award, Best Episodic Comedy ("The Mango"), 1995

Andy Ackerman

Directors Guild of America Award, Best Director of a Comedy Series ("The Rye"), 1997

Janet Ashikaga

Emmy Award, Outstanding Individual Achievement in Editing for a Series/Multicamera Production, 1992, 1994, 1995

Tom Cherones

Directors Guild of America Award, Best Director of a Comedy Series ("The Contest"), 1993

Meg Liberman/Marc Hirschfeld

Casting Society of America Aritos Award, Best Casting in a Comedy Series, 1995

David Mandel

Writers Guild of America Award, Best Episodic Comedy ("The Pool Guy"), 1997

Elaine Pope/Larry Charles

Emmy Award, Outstanding Individual Achievement in Writing in a Comedy Series ("The Fix Up"), 1992

Writing for *Seinfeld*: Tips From an Insider

Seinfeld coproducer Peter Mehlman lived out the dream of many aspiring writers. A former free-lance magazine writer who also worked for the *Washington Post* and ABC Sports, Mehlman one day decided to write a *Seinfeld* script. He got an agent and sent the script to Larry David and Jerry Seinfeld.

The duo liked his work so much that they invited him to join the writing staff, where he eventually became coproducer. His scripts include "The Nose Job," "The Implant," and "The Smelly Car." And although the show rarely accepts unsolicited scripts (none is accepted without an agent), Mehlman shared some of his insights with aspiring television writers in 1994 at an Austin Writers' League seminar in Austin, Texas.

Five guidelines for writing a good *Seinfeld* script:

1. Make story lines reality-based and personal (the more embarrassing the better).
2. Hit an issue straight on—try to get as many laughs out of it as possible, without being too offensive.

3. Do not reveal any lessons at the end—nothing positive and nothing life-affirming.
4. Include a lot of lying and a lot of scheming.
5. Refer to incidents from previous episodes.

Abbott and Costello Meet Jerry and George

As a child growing up in Massapequa, Long Island, Jerry Seinfeld was introduced to Bud Abbott and Lou Costello through reruns of *The Abbott and Costello Show* on Channel 11. The show, which starred the pair as out-of-work actors sharing an apartment, made a lasting impression.

Abbott and Costello had such a great chemistry, observed Seinfeld in *Abbott and Costello Meet Jerry Seinfeld*, a 1994 NBC special devoted to the classic comedy team, that decades later their jokes and routines are still getting laughs.

And this great chemistry—captured forever in their forty-year-old show—has been a source of inspiration, ironically, for one of the defining shows of the 1990s. "I grew up on these two guys," said Seinfeld. "I loved them more than anything," he told Bill Carter of the *New York Times*.

Seinfeld even credits the team as a seminal influence on his life. "Watch-

---

How to Succeed as a TV Writer Without Really Trying

Larry David, Larry Charles, and Peter Mehlman offered these bits of advice to aspiring television writers at the Museum of TV and Radio's ninth annual Television Festival in Los Angeles:
- Don't take classes.
- Don't watch TV.
- Don't know somebody.

ing Abbott and Costello was one of the things that really got me interested in humor as a child," he once said. "It was the purest humor. Sitcoms and stuff weren't really pure. This was burlesque- and vaudeville-based style."

While most vaudeville comedians drew from a pool of two hundred classic routines, only Abbott and Costello's renditions of these skits survived, through their TV shows, films, and radio tapes, and the pair are responsible for preserving the entire genre.

"This is the history of the American style of comedy," Seinfeld said. "It's a unique American art form."

Like hundreds of other shows, much of the humor in *Seinfeld* can be traced back to Abbott and Costello's perfectly polished vaudeville bits. The duo's mix of precise execution and ad-libbing are "the roots of virtually every comedian you see working," Seinfeld revealed.

"Everybody on the show knows I'm a fan," he told the *New York Times*. "We're always joking about how we do stuff from *their* show. George and I will often get into a riff that has the rhythm from the old Abbott and Costello shows. And sometimes I'll hit George in the chest the way Abbott would hit Costello."

Jerry says George's middle name, "Louis," is a reference to Costello. "Sid Fields," Bud and Lou's fictional landlord, is also the name of the title character in *Seinfeld*'s "The Old Man." Another parallel between *Seinfeld* and the 1951–52 classic program is that both incorporate material based on the stars' personal experiences; both deal with showbiz personalities looking for work. Coincidentally, Channel 11, which used to broadcast the Abbott and Costello reruns of Jerry's youth, is currently broadcasting *Seinfeld* reruns in the New York metropolitan area.

The comic genius of Abbott *(right)* and Costello, preserved forever in film, had a lasting influence on young Jerry Seinfeld. (Starchives)

"We've always taken little bits that reminded us of Abbott and Costello in ways that only we would notice," Seinfeld told an interviewer. "Little turns and attitudes Jason [Alexander] and I try to do."

Comic duos back in the vaudeville days split the money 60-40, with the straight man getting the larger share and top billing—and justly so, said Seinfeld.

"With a great straight man, you had an act," he explained. "For my money, [Abbott] was the greatest straight man in show business history.

"When we talk about Abbott and Costello, most of the comedians I know talk about Bud," he explained. "That was the real expertise. As great as Costello was—and he was obviously a brilliant comedian—you don't see 'straight' work like Bud's anywhere. The form is pretty dead at this point."

In "The Subway," writer Larry Charles, another Abbott and Costello devotee, borrows a play on words from their classic "mudder-fadder" bit, in which Bud launches a hilarious repartee by selecting a racehorse based on his ability to run in muddy conditions.

"Bazooka," Bud says, "he's a good mudder."

"How can a *he* be a *mudder*?" replies Lou, setting off the sketch.

"To me, comedically they were very sophisticated," Seinfeld commented. "Abbott and Costello did intricate word play."

Their trademark skit, "Who's on First," in which Bud tries to explain to a befuddled Lou that a baseball team has players named "Who," "What," and "I Don't Know," "is constructed like the Eiffel Tower," Seinfeld said.

"Isn't it perfectly understandable that someone might get a little mixed up trying to comprehend this situation?" Seinfeld asked his TV-special audience. "Doesn't it almost seem as if this entire discussion has been specifically designed from the outset just to confuse a perfectly innocent human being?"

On *Seinfeld*, Jerry frequently plays the calm, cool straight man, leaving many of the funniest lines to Kramer, George, and Elaine. ("How many times have you heard me start a bit with the line, 'Now let me get this straight'?" he asks). But when George gets into scheming, Jerry gladly changes sides to assume the role of the lost, confused Lou. In "The Pitch," for example, George tries to explain the concept for a show about nothing:

JERRY: You want to go with me to NBC?
GEORGE: Yea. I think we really got something here.
JERRY: What do we got?
GEORGE: An idea.
JERRY: What idea?
GEORGE: An idea for the show.
JERRY: I still don't know what the idea is!
GEORGE: It's about nothing.
JERRY: Right.

In "The Tape," George tells Jerry that he's attracted to Elaine, but he cannot tell Jerry that Elaine left an erotic message on the comedian's tape recorder.

JERRY: Does she know?
GEORGE: No.
JERRY: How did it happen?
GEORGE: I can't say.
JERRY: Well, why can't you say?

Foul-ups and Cliffhangers

Just try to run an implausible story line past dedicated *Seinfeld* fans and they'll be ranting for days. Such was the case with "The Fusilli Jerry," in which Jerry learns that his mechanic, David, is using his patented "move" in bed on Elaine. When Jerry demands he stop using the "stolen" move, Elaine tells him she had always liked the move when Jerry used it back when they were dating.

But wait a minute . . . didn't Elaine claim in "The Mango" that she had "faked it" every time? Something seems amiss: If Jerry had used the move, maybe Elaine wouldn't have had to commit what Jerry calls "sexual perjury" back then? Needless to say, discussions raged at workplace water coolers and on the Internet for days.

While most goofs—known as continuity errors—occur in the writing stage (as appears to have happened in "The Fusilli Jerry"), they can also occur in the editing process. When episodes are shot, they rarely come in at the desired length. Often the editors have to pare twenty-eight or thirty minutes of footage down to the twenty-two-minute program length. And in doing this, some things are bound to be fouled up. However, the folks at *Seinfeld* should have known something as important as Elaine's orgasms were not going to be overlooked!

Seinfeld has left several other burning questions unanswered. Many would like to know what happened to . . .

Kramer's Offspring

In "The Chinese Woman," Kramer visits a fertility clinic in order to get his sperm count

GEORGE: Because I promised her.

JERRY: I thought you just said she doesn't know.

GEORGE: She doesn't.

JERRY: So how can you promise her?

GEORGE: Because she asked me to.

JERRY (finally breaking down): "What is this—an Abbott and Costello routine?"

up so he can someday pass along the Kramer name. At the episode's conclusion, he leans out the window and exclaims to Jerry that his girlfriend, Noreen, is late ("She's laaaatee!!!"). But we never found out if Kramer did manage to "slip one past the goalie" or if it was just a false alarm. Kramer had previously picked out a name for his son—Isosceles—in "The Handicap Spot."

The Greenpeace Guy

In "The Pilot," Larry David set up *Seinfeld* for a *Crying Game*–type scenario when a Greenpeace activist tells drowning ex–NBC president Russell Dalrymple that he will find Elaine and "tell her all about you and what you did out here." Never happened!

Ricky, the *TV Guide* fanatic

What ever happened to Ricky? The psychotic TV-watcher was smitten with Elaine in "The Cigar Store Indian" after he spotted her on the subway reading "the *Guide*" so far away from the television. He was briefly seen in "The Pie" as the creator of the TR-6 mannequin (aka "Elaine"), which was getting "spanked" by another mannequin in a department store window, but never heard from again.

Whither Babu?

If, for some reason, the show wants to bump off Jerry, Pakistani restaurateur Babu Bhatt might be the man to do it. Through a typically Seinfeldian turn of events in "The Visa," Jerry, George, Elaine, and Kramer all contribute to Babu's deportation from the U.S. Back in Pakistan, Babu vows: "Someday I will get back to America, and when I do, I will exact vengeance on this man. I cannot forget him—he haunts me. He is a very bad man. He is a very, very bad man."

Bathroom Humor

No one who has seen Jerry's stand-up act would accuse him of using "bathroom humor" (he said using four-letter words in comedy is like cooking with Hamburger Helper). So why do so many of *Seinfeld*'s laughs emanate from the lavatory? Consider these examples:

Riffing on Rifkin

Elaine was not the only one anguished by her relationship with a Joel Rifkin in 1993's "The Masseuse" episode.

Jeanne Rifkin, the real-life mother of the confessed Long Island serial killer, happened to be watching the show—and she was not amused, according to her son's lawyer.

"[She] saw it and was very upset," attorney John Lawrence told the New York *Daily News*.

In the episode, Elaine becomes self-conscious after coworkers tease her about her boyfriend's infamous name. Even strangers raise eyebrows when they hear him paged at a New York Giants game. "He's not the murderer," Elaine says timidly.

The lawyer for the real Joel Rifkin felt the situation was inappropriate for a comedy series. "Considering the gravity of the situation, I'd like to keep it in the confines of the court," he said.

In the show, Elaine finally convinces Joel to change his first name so he will not be identified with a murderer. Ironically, one of the names on her list of alternates is . . . O.J. "O.J. Rifkin," she exclaims. "Oh, please, please, please change your name to O.J.! Please. It would be so great!"

- George says he always removes his shirt when he's visiting "the office" ("The Gymnast").
- Heeding nature's call, Kramer bolts out of his audition with NBC to find a bathroom. After an unsuccessful search of the city, he runs home to his "home base" only to discover he's lost his "peristalsis" ("The Pilot").
- George quits his job at the real estate firm because the boss won't let George use his private bathroom ("The Revenge").
- George follows his girlfriend Nina, a model he is dating, into a restaurant ladies' room to find out if she's been "refunding" the dinners he is paying for ("The Switch").

• Jerry complains that a mall has six hundred stores "and I didn't see one bathroom." He and George are later ticketed by a security guard for urinating in the parking garage ("The Parking Garage").

• Kramer kicks open a bathroom stall door and snaps a Polaroid of his accountant on the toilet ("The Sniffing Accountant").

• George is caught urinating in the shower at his health club ("The Wife").

• A woman in a movie-theater restroom refuses to "spare a square" of toilet paper for a desperate Elaine in the adjoining stall. When Elaine finds out it was Jane, Jerry's girlfriend, she gets revenge on her by stealing the toilet paper from the bathroom at Monk's Diner ("The Stall").

• Poppie urinates on Jerry's new couch in retaliation for his having caused a disturbance at his restaurant ("The Couch"). Poppie gives a "repeat performance" after George and Jerry leave the same couch in the lobby of Mr. Pitt's building ("The Doorman").

• George cuts short his first intimate encounter with Tatiana because of an "impending intestinal requirement" and leaves her apartment because her bathroom does not provide him with the privacy that he needs ("The Chinese Restaurant").

Trouble at the Ballpark

Although Jerry's real-life trips to ballparks have been pleasurable experiences (he often sneaks into the broadcast booths to liven up the pre-game show and tours new stadiums) the same can't be said for his TV counterpart and his friends when they're around baseball.

For example, Elaine was ejected twice from New York Yankees owner George Steinbrenner's box at Yankee Stadium for wearing an Orioles cap

Moops Mystery Solved!

One astute *Seinfeld* fan has come up with a possible theory to explain one of the show's funniest buzzwords: Moops.

The episode was "The Bubble Boy," and in it, the title character, Donald, engages George in a game of Trivial Pursuit. With the game hanging in the balance, George asks the Bubble Boy this potentially deciding question: "Who invaded Spain in the eighth century?"

"That's a joke," says the Bubble Boy, confident of a win over his bald visitor. "The Moors."

"Oh nooooo," replies George, doing his disappointed Alex Trebek imitation. "I'm so sorry. It's the Moops."

"Moops!?! Lemme see that. That's not *Moops*, you jerk—it's *Moors*. It's a misprint!"

In the ensuing fracas that breaks out, George accidentally bursts the boy's bubble, causing a medical emergency that gets the whole town incensed.

"Well, it just so happens that I own a copy of the ninth edition of the *Jeopardy!* home game, which was issued in 1972," said *Seinfeld* fan Leslie E. Frates, a lecturer at California State University–Hayward. "*Double Jeopardy!* Game #16 contains this $100 answer-question combination under the category of Columbus:

ANSWER: Only after she defeated them could Isabella consider Columbus's requests.
QUESTION: Who are the Moops?

"Gentlemen and ladies of the jury," Frates said to an audience of Internet surfers, "I submit that Larry Charles and Larry David, the writers of the episode, also own, or at least have played, the same *Jeopardy!* home game. The coincidence is just too weird!"

Frates even sent a letter about the coincidence to the show, but never received a reply.

Frates first came across the Moops mistake while studying for an appearance on the real *Jeopardy!*'s Tournament of Champions. Frates, who appeared on *Jeopardy!* more than any other woman—a total of ten times—recalled, "I laughed my head off then and once again when I saw the *Seinfeld* episode."

("The Letter"). Kramer, who complains that Steinbrenner is ruining his life by trading away all of the Yankees' best prospects ("The Smelly Car"), brings a baseball fantasy camp to a halt after "plunking" Yankee great Joe Pepitone for crowding the plate. Although the players were not seen in that episode, "The Visa," Kramer describes the ensuing melee with Mickey Mantle (whom he punched in the face) and other Yanks Moose Skowron, Clete Boyer, and Hank Bauer, who get caught up in the brouhaha. The ballpark even spells trouble for Jerry, who meets a future ex-girlfriend, Miss Rhode Island, at Yankee Stadium ("The Chaperone").

Even softball brings misfortune on *Seinfeld*, as in "The Understudy," when Jerry and George are accused of conspiring with a Broadway understudy (Jerry's gal, Gennise) to sideline Bette Midler, star of *Rochelle, Rochelle: The Musical*.

George fulfilled a dream by landing a job with the Yankees in "The Opposite," in which he acted contrary to everything his instincts told him. Part of acting opposite, *Seinfeld* fans may recall, was balling out Yankee owner George Steinbrenner (actually an actor in silhouette resembling The Boss) during a job interview. After taking over as assistant to the traveling secretary, George's biggest blunder was to replace the polyester uniforms with cotton ones. While the team finds them more comfortable, the uniforms shrink after one washing, and make the players run "like penguins." In another episode, George is accused of pilfering Yankee equipment and even Steinbrenner's vitamins ("The Jimmy"). Although he tends to be a slacker (and an inept one at that), George's allegiance will always be to the Bronx Bombers. He even suggests the name Seven for his first child (boy or girl) after the Yankees' Number Seven, Mickey Mantle.

Steinbrenner, already a character in the sports world, has been a willing subject of *Seinfeld* humor, having given permission for the parody. Seen from behind, seated at his desk in a huge oak-paneled office, the Steinbrenner character, played by actor Lee Baer, turns every meeting with George into nonsensical, rambling monologue (in a voice provided by Larry David). In one episode, he sends George to Cuba to check out a hot young player. But when George meets Fidel Castro, he finds the dictator to be a carbon copy of The Boss.

Rob Butcher, a spokesperson for the team, said The Boss has a pretty good sense of humor when it comes to these things. For the record, however, Steinbrenner would not kick anyone out of his box for wearing an Orioles cap—and there's no such job as assistant to the traveling secretary.

"They're very good, very funny, very well written," the real George Steinbrenner told the *New York Times*. "It's amazing how popular the show is. And my grandchildren love it. My oldest is nine years old, and he thinks being on that show is the greatest thing I've ever accomplished in my life. The writers are terrific. I'm impressed with the detail, even down to the names in the Yankees' parking lot. I was prepared not to like the show, but I came away laughing my head off."

Steinbrenner said his favorite episode is "The Caddy," in which The Boss tells the Costanzas that George is dead. "[Frank Costanza] hollers at me, 'How could you trade Buhner?' It was sick, but hilarious."

Larry David shares George Costanza's love for the team and his frustration with Steinbrenner, who has irritated fans, players, and managers with his overbearing management style. So it was a weird instance of life imitating art when the Steinbrenner character slips up in "The Wink" and announces that he's firing then-manager Buck Showalter in one of his rambling one-sided conversations. Just weeks after the episode aired, the real Boss gave Showalter the real boot!

Seinfeld Zaps "Blackout Thursday"

NBC thought it had a clever promotion on its hands when it dubbed Thursday, November 3, 1994, "Blackout Thursday." The plan was to have all of the network's Thursday night sitcoms revolve around a single event—a New York City power outage. Only one problem; the *Seinfeld* episode scheduled for that week, "The Gymnast," had already been filmed and edited by the time studio honchos announced their idea.

Result? *Mad About You* and *Friends* kicked off the blackout concept at 8:00 and 8:30 P.M. respectively; *Seinfeld* came on (as did the lights) at 9:00; but then the power went out once more for *Madman of the People* at 9:30. Despite periodic "news breaks" by *Today* show weatherman (and *Seinfeld* guest star) Al Roker, NBC was left in the dark.

A similar scheme, "Star-Crossed Thursday," was hatched in the 1995–96 season, in which characters from *Friends*, *The Single Guy*, and *Caroline in the City* appeared on each other's shows.

The lack of a *Seinfeld* presence in the promotion was explained away by the star: "As you've probably noticed, we're not joiners," Jerry said. "For some reason, we're at the party but we're never really in the main group of people. We're the people making wisecracks over by the bad meat."

Although Jerry Seinfeld is a huge baseball fan, it's pretty clear he's more comfortable watching the game than playing it.

Seinfeld was once offered the chance to play for the Kinston (North Carolina) Indians, a Cleveland Indians farm club. Seems the right fielder at the time, Marc Marini, resembled Jerry and was even nicknamed "Seinfeld" by the team and their fans. But the team thought it would be funny to get the real Seinfeld out in right field.

In a letter, the Indians offered Seinfeld $1 to play right field at a home

Jerry's Favorite Player

When Jerry meets his baseball idol, Keith Hernandez, in "The Boyfriend," it seems to be a dream come true. But when Hernandez tries to move too fast in his friendship with Jerry—and his romance with Elaine—they both ask themselves, "Who does this guy think he is?" Well, here's the scoop:

Born: October 20, 1953, in San Francisco
Bats: Left
Throws: Left
Height: 6'
Weight: 205 lbs.
Nickname: "Mex"

Keith Hernandez played seventeen years in Major League Baseball, with the St. Louis Cardinals (1974–1983), the New York Mets (1983–1989), and the Cleveland Indians (1990). Known for his clutch hitting and exquisite fielding, Hernandez won the National League batting title in 1979 and was the league's co-MVP that same year. He played in six National League all-star games and won eleven consecutive Rawlings Gold Glove Awards for his unparalleled defense at first base (one broadcaster dubbed him "the Baryshnikov of first basemen"). He was a member of two World Championship teams: the 1982 Cardinals and the 1986 Mets. In his seventeen years of regular season play—2,088 games—Keith Hernandez achieved a Lifetime Batting Aver-

game for one pitched ball. Had he accepted, Seinfeld would have been officially entered on the all-time Cleveland Indians farm system compiled roster.

"He could spend the day in uniform, take batting practice, warm up our left fielder between innings, and even throw a little in the bullpen," explained the assistant general manager at the time, Billy Johnson. "The radio guys could say 'Jerry Seinfeld is now heating up for Kinston in the left field pen.' How many people would love to have that chance?"

age of .296, with 2,182 hits, 162 home runs, and 1,071 runs batted in.

Hernandez is the author of two books, *If at First: A Season With the Mets* (1985), and *Pure Baseball* (1994).

It was with the Mets that Hernandez participated in one of the most amazing games in baseball history—game six of the 1986 World Series. In this game, the Mets made a dramatic tenth-inning comeback against their opponents, the Boston Red Sox, to tie the series 3–3. The Mets went on to defeat Boston in the seventh and deciding game to become the World Champions. Ever since, "Game Six" has been the stuff of legend.

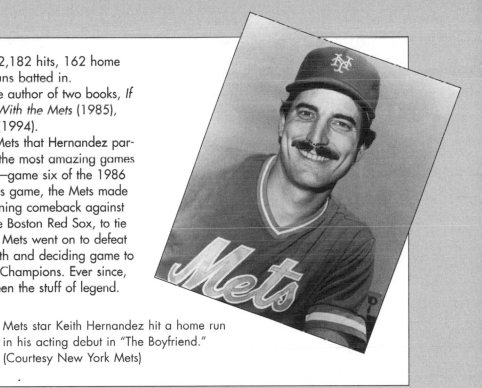

Mets star Keith Hernandez hit a home run in his acting debut in "The Boyfriend." (Courtesy New York Mets)

The team also recreated the July 8–22, 1993, *Rolling Stone* cover photo, which featured a leather-clad *Seinfeld* gang strutting their stuff.

"We figured that after Marc received national attention for looking like Seinfeld, maybe the next logical step was to develop a publicity photo," said Johnson, who, like Marini, has since left the team. "The timing of the *Rolling Stone* cover story featuring Seinfeld's program was just too good to pass up."

Although the team had their fingers crossed, Seinfeld never took them up on their offer, said a spokesperson.

Seinfeld in Commercials

When *Seinfeld* made the jump to the top ten in 1993, it wasn't just the viewers taking notice. Madison Avenue began to see the four actors as its key to reaching the demographically desirable—but cynical—young adult generation.

This group, consisting of older Generation-Xers and young Baby Boomers, is the most media savvy yet and potentially the biggest spenders. Latching on to these fickle consumer groups, however, is tricky.

In order to link their products to the hit show, ad campaigns began to be created around the familiar characters. After all, if the brand wasn't lucky enough to get a mention on the show, the next best thing was to just hire Jerry, George, Elaine, or Kramer to do the ad.

Of course, plugs are not limited to commercial breaks. *Advertising Age* says a one-minute mention on a show like *Seinfeld* can be worth as much as $350,000. Calvin Klein was so delighted with the free publicity from *Seinfeld* (Kramer pitches his perfume idea in "The Pez Dispenser" and later claims a CK flunkie ripped off the idea in "The Pick") that he sent Michael Richards a year's supply of Eternity for Men.

So over the past few years, Madison Avenue has cast Jerry Seinfeld as an urban, self-assured, and successful bachelor. Jason Alexander plays the insecure underdog; Julia Louis-Dreyfus appears as a sensual, sassy working girl; and Michael Richards plays the oddball.

No matter who's doing the advertising, *Seinfeld* is hot, with advertisers gladly paying up to $500,000 in 1998 for a thirty-second spot in order to reach the 30 million fans, mostly educated, with enough income to dispose of on whatever is being sold.

New York Times advertising columnist Stuart Elliot asked in one of his popular twenty-questions pieces, "Now that the four leading cast members of the sitcom *Seinfeld* are moonlighting in commercials, will they record a sequel to the album *The Who Sell Out?*" The phenomenon includes the show's supporting characters as well, with George's parents (Estelle Harris and Jerry Stiller) engaged in a shouted dialogue for AT&T long distance service. Even David Letterman made a comment in one of his "new books" rou-

Jerry gets some pointers in Central Park before skating away to commercial success. (Gene Shaw/Star File)

tines. Letterman held up a new "six-hundred-page volume—the *Guide to TV Commercials Made by the Cast of* Seinfeld."

"Well," Julia rationalized, "it's not like the *Seinfeld* cast is selling nuclear weapons."

Here's what they are selling . . .

• The real Jerry Seinfeld is way ahead of his character—who was contacted to do TV spots for "Leapin' Larry's" electronics stores in "The Secret Code." In 1992, Seinfeld became the national spokesperson for American Express, focusing first on the "outrageous" interest rates charged by bank credit cards and getting viewers to take an application from the omnipresent displays.

Later, the commercials demonstrated how the card—with no preset spending limit—prepares one for life's unpredictable situations. In one spot, he falls over the railing of a cruise ship, washes up on a resort island, and uses the card for food, clothing, a hotel, a rental car, and a helicopter ride back to the ship. Another spot features Jerry on a date in an Italian restaurant. When his date's large Italian family shows up unexpectedly, the intimate dinner turns into a party. Jerry, irked but prepared, picks up the tab with the card. Yet another commercial finds Jerry locked out of his apartment in a bathrobe. With just minutes before his date is to arrive, he dashes across the street to buy a suit, pick up a bouquet of flowers, hire a jazz combo, and find a locksmith to let him back in. Of course, all of these merchants accept American Express. In his most recent spot, Jerry uses his AmEx card to scour New York City for a pair of lost Knicks tickets.

American Express and its agency, Ogilvy & Mather, trusted Jerry to come up with his own "comedic interpretations" of their message in order to appeal to his fans. Jerry's image—smart, sophisticated, and successful—helped the company achieve its goal of getting twenty-five- to thirty-five-year-olds to fill out applications.

Jerry Seinfeld eventually teamed up with his comic-book idol, Superman, for an American Express commercial that aired in early 1998. The ad was not just a dream come true for the comedian. In fact, the commercial, which combined live-action and animated footage, was Jerry's idea, and it instantly became an audience favorite.

• Although he has done commercials since the age of fourteen, Jason Alexander will probably be best remembered for his Rold Gold pretzel ads. Alexander plays a sort of underachiever who attributes sudden spurts of strength or courage to the pretzels—not unlike George might do. In fact, George is seen eating a bag of Rold Gold pretzels at Jerry's apartment in "The Glasses."

"We wanted to make Rold Gold seem more hip, and Jason has great appeal," said a company official. "In the spots, he makes the brand the hero."

Jason again played an insecure bachelor in a series of ads for the Intel videophone technology in which he used the high-tech computer device to set up dates with beautiful women—only to have his dream dates fall apart. In one ad, a date cancels after she sees Jason's shabby apartment on her videophone; in another, the woman sees Jason's hunky brother and falls in love with him instead.

• Perhaps the most effective commercials to feature a *Seinfeld* player are for Clairol's Nice 'N Easy hair coloring. Julia Louis-Dreyfus (who reportedly uses #121 Natural Deep Brown) "fits the brand's everywoman image and pokes fun at the vacuous beauty role to perfection," said ad critic Patricia Winters in the New York *Daily News.* "Plus, she has great

Jerry: 2
Rental Car Industry: 0

Car-rental executives knew they had public relations trouble when Jerry Seinfeld began dissecting their industry on national television. In one encounter ("The Airport"), he rents a car with a broken radio, a window that won't roll down, and the aroma of a cheap hooker. In "The Alternate Side," he spars with an unyielding counter agent.

According to *Travel Weekly*, someone at the annual American Car Rental Association convention in 1994 asked Budget Rent A Car exec William Plamondon if the industry has an image problem. He responded by showing a clip of *Seinfeld*'s "The Alternate Side."

In the clip, Jerry is dismayed to learn that despite the fact that he made a reservation, there are no midsize cars available. Executives got a good laugh until the end of the scene, when Jerry settles on a compact car and tells the agent, "You'd better give me the insurance because I'm going to beat the hell out of this car."

hair." In the ad, she claims, "I'm just one of those women who happens to have naturally beautiful hair . . . Look, this color, this shine, I'm so luckeeeee."

Asked what makes her hair so special, Louis-Dreyfus says, "I have absolutely no idea. All I know is it grows out of my head and I've never been particularly good at handling it."

• Michael Richards was leery of diving into the lucrative commercial pool with his castmates. "The money is staggering to me, really staggering," he once said. "But they would own me. I'm afraid to be associated as the guy

Opposite: Michael Richards blasts into character for one of his zany Pepsi ads. (Pepsi-Cola Company)

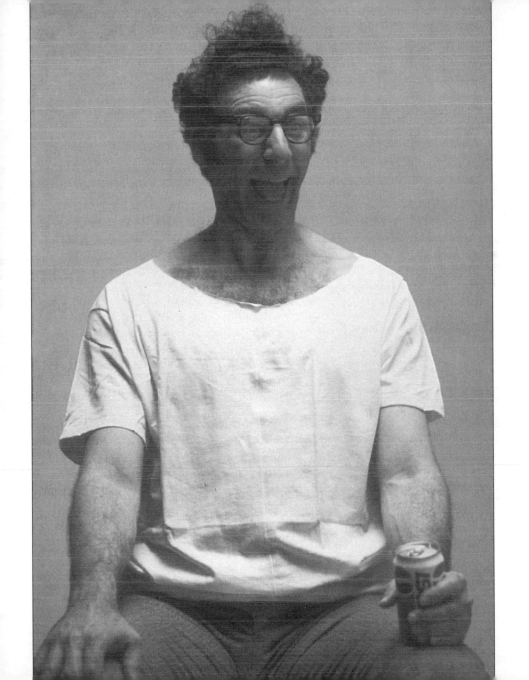

Move Over, Monk's

With its *Seinfeld*-inspired cuisine and decor, Bitterman's Deli, at 5 West Canon Perdido in downtown Santa Barbara, holds the distinction of being the only American monument to both eating and *Seinfeld*. The deli has become known among locals as "that *Seinfeld* deli" as well as by curious visitors, who stop by hoping to catch a favorite episode on the deli's TV set, which plays nothing but *Seinfeld* from morning till night. We decided to talk to the manager, Shawn Noormand, about this unusual theme.

When did you decide to go with the *Seinfeld* motif?

It was right when we opened—May of '93. We had 'em all on tape and we thought it would be a good idea to draw extra people here and get them familiar with the show. Since then, we've written letters to Castle Rock Entertainment, and they gave us permission to play the show, and we got a lot more people interested in watching the show. It helps us with business, and it helps the producers of the show because they get more people watching. We've gotten articles in some national magazines about us. It's been really popular.

I understand you have some *Seinfeld* specialties on the menu?

We have one named after each of the main characters, including Newman. Most of them are named after the people because at some time they ordered that sandwich in the show at the cafe—or it has to do with that person in the show.

The Jerry is a turkey club—he orders it a few times in different episodes. The Elaine is dolphin-safe tuna—she's always talking about how she's into Greenpeace and stuff like that. We have a Newman sandwich that's a skyscraper with corned beef and pastrami and cole slaw and Thousand Island dressing. It's huge.

How about George and Kramer?

The George is a ham and cheese, because George is just such a neurotic ham. The Kramer is a huge hot dog. In one of the shows he orders a Papaya King hot dog. He's got to have a Papaya King hot dog—not a movie hot dog.

What do the customers say about the ambiance?

They like it a lot. Most of the people come in and laugh out loud while they're watching the TV show and talking with their friends. We get a lot of people who come in by themselves and then bring their friends because they just can't believe that a place is playing this show all day long.

How long are you going to keep this up?

As long as our lease lasts, we'll continue playing the show. At least another four years.

Deli man Shawn Noormand displays a sandwich fit for the king of primetime comedy. (Todd Kaplan)

who sells a product. I want to be in this business for thirty years. I don't want to be a shooting star."

He apparently had a change of heart in 1994, when he debuted in the first of a series of Pepsi commercials during the Super Bowl. In the spots, Richards plays an oddball scientist, Dr. Leotard, who sets out to scientifically prove that Pepsi is the ultimate beverage. The first spot, "Deprivation Tank," showed what can happen when one goes too long without Pepsi (a Cindy Crawford can transform into a Rodney Dangerfield) and was ranked by *USA Today* as America's third favorite commercial during the game.

The campaign was eventually dropped, and Kramer—perhaps coincidentally—was seen sipping a Diet Coke in the 1994–95 *Seinfeld* season finale, "The Understudy."

Richards's other notable campaign was for the Orlando Magic in 1993–94, where he unleashed a little more of the Kramer persona. Standing alone in a blackened studio, Richards jumps, shouts, and clowns with a basketball while describing the action during a Magic game. Rapid cuts and Richards's own in-your-face energy help convey the feeling of a frenzied fan watching a Shaquille O'Neal slam-dunk: "Then there's the incredible alley-oop to Shaq," Richards shouts. "And ka-pow! Good-bye backboard!"

In 1996, Richards starred in a sexy Mercedes commercial with a woman who looked a lot like Elaine Benes.

In 1998, Richards was back in the Super Bowl telecast, this time turning in a maniacally fast-paced performance pitching Tommy Hilfiger sportswear.

Episodes: Five for the Ages

Comedian Dennis Miller perhaps put it best when he said *Seinfeld* is the one show "that I definitely feel should be loaded into the time capsule as the best our generation has to offer."

But since all those tapes would crowd the capsule, we might recommend that these five episodes be the ones preserved for the ages:

1. "The Contest"
Original air date: November 18, 1992
Written by: Larry David

One of *Seinfeld*'s predominant themes is that all the learning one does in one's life will still not prepare him for every situation. Such was the case in "The Contest," where George is caught by his mother in his parents' house, "treating his body like it was an amusement park." As George describes the embarrassing incident at the diner, he vows never again to masturbate. The other three then decide to make a competition to see who can go the longest without self-gratification.

Of course, the beauty of the whole episode, which won an Emmy for writer Larry David, is that the characters carefully avoided the *m*-word, so that anyone not paying attention—or tuning in late—would miss the subject of the wager.

"We never use that word," Julia Louis-Dreyfus once explained, "which is part of the reason it worked."

It is remarkable that Elaine was even allowed in—just like the rest of the boys. While she had to ante up $150 to the guys' $100, it was rare to see TV treat male urges and female urges on the same level.

" 'The Contest' was sheer bliss," Louis-Dreyfus said. "It was unusual material and I was happy to be included. It's funny to think of it as groundbreaking."

"We always make good shows," Jerry Seinfeld told *USA Today*. "You can only make it really good, and sometimes it jumps into great. The ones that have become really great kind of do it on their own. We didn't know 'The Contest' would be what it was. We just thought it would be another show. We don't know sometimes until we put them on the air."

Most people put this episode in the category "could be controversial." It did, in fact, spark a protest from right-wing Reverend Donald Wildmon's American Family Association, but the effort dissipated rather quickly.

Historical notes: While Kramer is the first to be out, and Elaine loses her title Queen of the Castle, the outcome of the battle between Jerry (Lord of the Manor) and George (King of the County) is left hanging in this episode. The winner of the contest is obliquely and offhandedly revealed the following season in "The Puffy Shirt," when George, working as a hand model, reassures his employer that he won't strain his hands the way his predecessor did. "You don't have to worry about me," George says, "I won a contest."

While the story is based on a real-life competition that involved Larry David and his friends, Jason Alexander admits he drew on some personal experiences in this episode as well.

"I actually did get caught," Alexander recalled in an interview, "not in a masturbation thing. But when I was eighteen, my girlfriend and I were at it pretty hot and heavy in the back seat of a car when a cop threw a light in there. That was no fun. I lost a little more than hair that evening."

2. "The Boyfriend"
Original air date: February 12, 1992
Written by: Larry David and Larry Levin

Jerry courts the friendship of former Mets star Keith Hernandez, who is interested in Elaine. While they both begin "dating" Hernandez, neither relationship works out. Elaine dumps him because he smokes; Jerry breaks it off because he feels Keith is moving the relationship too fast (by asking him to help move his stuff to a new apartment only a few days into the friendship).

The highlight of the show finds Kramer and Newman explaining the reason they hate Keith Hernandez: he once spit at Kramer, hitting Newman as well, after a baseball game. An investigation by Jerry determines that their "magic loogie" theory simply does not hold up; Keith could not have done it—there had to have been a "second spitter."

Jerry's "magic loogie" demonstration, an homage to Oliver Stone's film *JFK* (in which Wayne Knight plays one of Jim Garrison's men), even includes a grainy, faded eight-millimeter re-creation of the infamous Zapruder film of the Kennedy assassination. This clever remake includes such *JFK* ingredients as the "umbrella man" in the background and a con-spirator (relief pitcher Roger McDowell) behind some bushes over by the "gravely road."

During the filming of the episode it was clear that it was running between a half hour and an hour. NBC had been asking Seinfeld and David to come up with a full hour anyway, so David made the call to stretch the show to an hour with some additional Seinfeld stand-up material.

The show was a treat for Jerry, whose real-life fascination with Hernan-dez is evidenced by the photo of him on the apartment wall (near the window). Julia says she "got to kiss Keith—and that makes it one of my favorite shows too."

The producers were proud of the fact that Hernandez pulled off the episode despite having had no prior acting experience "other than protest-ing a third strike."

3. "The Chinese Restaurant"
Original air date: May 23, 1991
Written by: Larry David and Jerry Seinfeld

When *Washington Post* TV critic Tom Shales called *Seinfeld* "painfully amusing and amusingly painful," he was probably referring to episodes like "The Chinese Restaurant." In this one, Jerry, George, and Elaine wait for a table at a Chinese restaurant before a showing of Ed Wood Jr.'s *Plan 9 From Outer Space*, universally hailed as the worst movie of all time.

Elaine is famished, George is waiting to use a pay phone to make an important call, and Jerry knows one of the restaurant patrons will catch him in a lie that got him out of a dinner engagement with his uncle.

The trio sees one party after another seated, while the maître d' keeps assuring them "five, ten minutes." They leave just before their party is called for a table.

Historical note: Jerry and George try to sell this very story to NBC as an example of their "show about nothing."

When Jerry at one point is confronted with seeing the movie by himself, he whines "I can't go to a bad movie by myself—what am I, going to make sarcastic remarks to strangers?" This was most likely a nod to Joel Hodgson, cowriter of Jerry's 1987 HBO special, *Stand-Up Confidential*, and original host of Comedy Central's *Mystery Science Theater 3000*, a show that mocked bad cinema.

Kramer is not in this episode, but five years later, in "The Postponement," Jerry describes the incident to him and asks him if he'd like to see *Plan 9* at a movie theater. It is at this screening that Kramer scalds himself with a caffe latte he smuggled into the theater in his pants.

What's "The" Deal?

The only regular episode that doesn't start off with "The" in the title is "Male Unbonding," which originally aired June 14, 1990. Why there's no "The" and why this is significant to this author is "an enigma wrapped in a riddle."

4. "The Parking Garage"
Original air date: October 30, 1991
Written by: Larry David

The *Seinfeld* team says God deserves a writing credit for this episode, in which the characters travel to a New Jersey mall so Kramer can get a good price on an air conditioner. After he buys it, the gang looks for his car but can't remember where they parked. To make matters worse, Jerry has to go to the bathroom, George is running late for his parents' anniversary celebration, and Elaine is worried that the goldfish she has just bought will die in its plastic bag.

After a grueling half-hour of wandering (the viewer starts to feel tired too), they finally find the car and get in. But when Michael Richards turned the ignition key, the script got some divine intervention: the battery had died and the car wouldn't start. A perfect ending to thirty minutes of nothing.

"The original ending was that we were driving around and we couldn't find the exit," Julia Louis-Dreyfus would later recall. "At three o'clock in the morning, that particular shoot was very difficult for many reasons, and we shot into the wee hours of the morning. And the last shot was in fact the final shot of the show—we were supposed to climb into the car and go.

"And when we did, Michael couldn't start the car. It actually wouldn't start. It was like God had actually given us a better ending to the script. We were laughing so damn hard that if you watch that episode, you can see—I think it's Jason and me in the back seat, and our heads are bobbing, trying to stop our hysterical laughter, trying to keep it under control while the camera's running."

Along with "The Chinese Restaurant," "The Parking Garage" is a prime example of what Barbara Walters meant when she said, "The less the show is about, the better it seems to be."

Technical note: Contrary to popular belief, "The Parking Garage" was shot not in an actual mall but at a huge set constructed in CBS's Studio City. Director Tom Cherones shot the one set to look as if the characters had walked through several different levels.

5. "The Subway"
Original air date: January 8, 1992
Written by: Larry Charles

Unlike the proverbial nothingness of "The Parking Garage" and "The Chinese Restaurant," plenty happens in "The Subway," the best example of how *Seinfeld* weaves together four credible, and hilarious, subplots into one cohesive half-hour.

After breakfast at Monk's, the gang descends into the subway, where each one boards a different train.

Jerry, on his way to the car pound, wakes up from a subway doze to find a naked man seated across from him. They strike up a conversation about baseball and eventually make friends, go to Nathan's, and ride the Cyclone at Coney Island.

George, meanwhile, is conned by a would-be seductress who takes him to a hotel, handcuffs him to a bed, and makes off with his money (eight bucks) and his suit.

Subway delays derail Elaine's chance to be the "best man" at a lesbian wedding, and Kramer overhears a horse tip on his train. Instead of paying off his $600 in parking tickets, he puts the money on a 30-to-1 longshot and wins a bundle.

They all end up—where else?—in the diner.

"The ones I really like are when you twist stories in unexpected ways and yet still manage to twirl them into a point at the end," Seinfeld would later say.

Technical note: The whole episode utilized only one subway-car set, shot from different angles.

The Man Behind the Music

While the *Seinfeld* TV show has often been called "offbeat," that description could certainly apply to the show's theme music as well. To come up with a score that complemented the wacky exploits of the *Seinfeld* gang, Jerry tapped Jonathan Wolff of the Music Consultants Group in Burbank, California, whose TV scoring credits include dozens of shows, such as *Who's the Boss?*, *Married With Children*, *Knots Landing*, and *21 Jump Street*.

"We worked together on the type of sound that it would be," Jerry Seinfeld told *Entertainment Tonight*. "And he put in the lip-popping. I really liked that. He does a great job."

Wolff suggested using unconventional "alternate" sounds instead of the usual drums and trumpets. Currently, he works from a palate of five hundred sounds, including lip pops, sighs, gasps, and other noises Wolff "performs" and records himself in a sound booth. Using a computer and a synthesizer, Wolff is able to play the unconventional sounds on a synthesizer, along with his other "samples," which include the more recognizable slap-bass and horns. All the sounds are then strung together to form melodies.

"Generally, the music for the monologue starts very quietly," Wolff said, making the "chicka-chicka-chicka-chicka" noise. "We call that 'The Shaker.' "

From there, Wolff's music becomes an offscreen counterpart to Jerry and his friends. His tunes are used to change scenes, accent a weird plot twist, or end the show with a bang after a big payoff.

Each half-hour episode takes Wolff six hours to score, but he seems to enjoy the work. "It's amazing to me that I get to do this," he said. "I would do this if they didn't pay me."

Meet Jerry Seinfeld

"**I** certainly never imagined at fifteen, when I started writing down these funny thoughts that kept coming into my head, that someday they would amount to a book," said Jerry Seinfeld in the introduction to his book, *Sein-Language.* "I never thought they would amount to anything, really."

But the funny thoughts, and the funny man behind them, is now on top of the world. With a hit TV show and a bestselling book under his belt, Seinfeld still sells out auditoriums across the country to people who pay to hear his unique spin on everything from laundry detergent to sex. For people who can't get enough, Seinfeld even makes TV commercials fun to watch.

"I never needed to be this successful. Never," he told Jane Pauley. "I was just happy that I could do comedy and not work. In fact, that was the hardest thing for me to adjust to—doing the series. It was that I was going to *work* in the *morning.* I wanted to scream to people, 'I'm not one of you, you know. I'm not just working.'

"I really was embarrassed," he continued. " 'Cause my whole life up to that point, me and my friends who were comedians, we would hang out during the day. We used to go down Sixth Avenue and watch everybody

At the time of his high school graduation, a young Jerry Seinfeld had aspirations of becoming a comic like Robert Klein or Bill Cosby. (Seth Poppel Yearbook Archives)

come out to lunch and [say] 'Go back! Go back to your buildings. Lunch hour is over! We're staying out.' It was just playing hooky. It was prolonging youth."

Born in Brooklyn on April 29, 1954, Seinfeld moved with his family to Massapequa, Long Island, when he was in the fifth grade. He enjoyed watching comedians like Red Skelton, Jonathan Winters, the Smothers Brothers, and others who'd appear on *The Ed Sullivan Show*. Other staples of his TV diet included *The Bullwinkle Show*, *Jonny Quest*, *Spider-Man*, *Batman*, *Flipper* . . . and reruns of *The Abbott and Costello Show*, whose reality-based humor had a lasting effect.

Jerry recalls being a "consistent laugh-getter" in school ("It was important to me. It still is.") and his third-grade teacher wrote in a report card, "Jerry does a little too much fooling around in class and not enough constructive activity."

While all kids observe life's peculiar moments, Jerry told Barbara Walters, "I didn't stop doing that. I didn't want to grow up. I wanted to keep doing that."

Jerry didn't care much for Long Island ("not enough action," he insists) and took a liking to comedy in his teens. He was enraptured with the only two stand-ups whom he would refer to as inspirations: Robert Klein, who pioneered the intelligent, observational stand-up comedy style, and Bill Cosby, whose mastery at unspooling a long, funny story had audiences hanging on to his every word.

In his early teens, Seinfeld began tape recording humorous interviews with his parakeet. An early girlfriend recalled that one of Jerry's bits at the time included John Wayne imitating a chicken.

"There were quite a few years there where I didn't really have any friends around the neighborhood," Seinfeld told Walters. "And that's when I started to be funny—that's what makes you funny—you have to use your own mind to keep yourself entertained."

Jerry says he picked up his timing from his late father, Kal, a self-employed sign painter who often took Jerry along on business calls. His mother, Betty, and sister, Carolyn, have stated that Kal was the funniest in the family, with a natural style—as opposed to Jerry's meticulously rehearsed style. Kal, who used charm and humor to sell signs, also had another profound effect on his son. "I'd ride in the van with my sneakers up on the dashboard," Seinfeld wrote in *SeinLanguage*, "and it was there that I first learned one of life's great pleasures, watching other people work."

With his parents' encouragement, Jerry began hanging around Manhattan comedy clubs, performing for little, if any, money. For Jerry, who claims he was not the outgoing type, performing was "absolute terror" at first. Many nights he wouldn't even get a shot on stage. It was his father who would often meet Jerry in the family kitchen at 3 or 4 A.M. after Jerry's commute back from the clubs via Long Island Railroad. Yet he stayed on his self-assigned "mission," working clubs and taking up theater and communications at Queens College. He even convinced a professor to give him credit for pursuing an independent study in stand-up.

"I remember in college, everybody talking about how they were going to get jobs," he told an interviewer. "I thought, 'Geez, I don't want to get a job. That doesn't seem like any fun. I've been having fun. I want to keep having fun.' So I said, 'Is there some sort of job out there where you can just fool around and have fun?' " Jerry even remembers thinking at the time, "I don't care if I starve, but I don't want to go to work."

The day he graduated from Queens College, on both the dean's list and honor roll, Seinfeld headed into Manhattan for another shot onstage. The very next day he took a job peddling jewelry on the streets of Manhattan and trying to evade police. Another less-than-glamorous job followed: selling light bulbs over the phone. When that job ended, Jerry waited tables at a Manhattan Brew and Burger, still concentrating his energy on the clubs. But by this time, he was an emcee one night a week at the Comic Strip, a popular Manhattan club.

"To be a comedian, I knew it was difficult," he recalled. "I said, 'Let me get jobs that are so bad that I'll be propelled to succeed as a comedian to get out of this hideous work.' "

When he got a second night as emcee at the Comic Strip, Seinfeld quit waiting tables, convinced he had been accepted as a professional comedian. His pay at that time was thirty-five dollars a night—seventy dollars a week.

"I turned in the apron," he recalled in *Playboy*. "I went out to visit my parents. I remember standing on the platform of the Long Island Railroad in Massapequa. That was the highest moment of my career. I was a comedian. I had made it . . . That was the transition from man to superman."

But on a bill with six or eight other comedians, Jerry had to quickly develop a style that would set him apart from the hordes of comics who performed the familiar girlfriend jokes or used gimmicks. His persona then, as now, was simply being himself on stage (although perhaps a little more forceful), pointing out the absurdities to be found in everyday life and vocalizing the things that most people let slip into their subconscious.

"I'm not as interested in the world, per se, as most people," he explained to Barbara Walters. "Some people look at a newspaper and see stories. I see the paper, and the ink, and the way it's folded."

"Some people are better at finding the humor in large issues that confront society," Larry David told *Rolling Stone* in 1994. "Jerry can go in, take a microscope, and examine the tiniest moments and see the humor in it."

On stage, Jerry blends the observational style of Klein with the timing of Cosby, forcing audiences to see the world through his eyes, then giving them time to think over his material and agree with him. His job, as he sees it, is to start a ripple effect in the audience, and then ride the wave of laughter like a surfer.

"That wave can crush you at any time," he once explained. "But while you're doing your maneuvering, you look like you're in control—but you're really not. The audience is always stronger."

Jerry's act got funnier and funnier, but harder to describe or categorize. He had no opening bit, no closing bit, and no "hook." No props, no impersonations, no screaming, no physical comedy. Nothing.

"I'm not 'that guy that . . . ,' " Seinfeld once explained. "I'm 'that guy.' "

In 1980, armed with the comedian's requisite twenty-five minutes of material, he headed for Los Angeles. He was already a road veteran, caught up in the eighties comedy boom, traveling as many as three hundred days a year.

Although Kal passed away in 1985, before the great success of *Seinfeld*, he did live to see Jerry reach a milestone for young comics: he saw him appear on *The Tonight Show Starring Johnny Carson* on May 7, 1981. Kal even painted a sign on the side of a truck and drove it around the neighborhood to advertise the event. Jerry's appearance, it turned out, was only the first of thirty with Carson.

"That's a great feeling for a son to know that you've fulfilled an ambition of your father's," Seinfeld remembered. Kal's presence is still felt on the *Seinfeld* set: a store called Kal Signs is part of the street scenery.

The exposure on the Carson show rocketed Jerry into the upper echelon of stand-up comedy. His schedule was still as busy, but the clubs—and the paychecks—got bigger.

His success in comedy, he said, was prompted by what drives success in other fields: talent, brains, and, most important, confidence. But it doesn't hurt that Seinfeld has a cold, logical approach to comedy that would make *Star Trek*'s Mr. Spock happy.

"I was great at geometry," Seinfeld said. "If I wanted to train someone as a comedian, I would make them do lots of proofs. That's what comedy is: a kind of bogus proof. You set up a fallacious premise and then prove it with rigorous logic. It just makes people laugh. You'll find that most of my stuff is based on that system . . . You must think very rationally on a completely absurd plane."

However, there's no textbook way to learn the comedy business. Seinfeld's best advice: write every day, perform every night, and don't care what happens to you. As he once told an audience, "It's like if you wanted to be a surgeon and someone said, 'Well, here's the knife. Start cutting the guy up—and keep cuttin' till the guy feels better.' "

Seinfeld has so much material to work with because despite the current information society, "seventy-five percent of the world is not touched on except by comedians." He's also constantly observing the world through two eyes and a comedic "third eye," roving for material.

"I'm annoyed," he confessed to *Playboy*. "But if you're not cranky and annoyed, you can't be a comedian. Any good comedian is, by definition, highly irritable. Even I, though I may not seem to be, am constantly irritated."

"There's nothing in life that I haven't thought about," he told *Rolling Stone*.

"Any time you get upset—your little comedy light goes off," he once explained.

Nothing sets off that light like New York City, where a struggling Seinfeld lived in a West Side studio apartment and a successful Jerry currently maintains a luxury apartment overlooking Central Park.

"I thrive on all the craziness," he told *Life*. "That's why New York produces good comedians. It's that constant chafing. If you've got a comedic bent, New York's going to provide you with plenty of ammo. The place is a gymnasium of irritation."

He calls the city "the greatest center of smartasses" and subscribes to the Frank Sinatra philosophy that says if you can make it there, you can make it anywhere. "Smooth seas make poor sailors," Seinfeld stated.

One source of material noticeably absent from his routine is his heritage. Although *Seinfeld* has Jewish elements (witness "The Bris" and Uncle Leo's ability to find anti-Semitism behind the smallest annoyances in life), Jerry has chosen not to make his ethnicity an issue on the show—or in his stand-up act ("I'm more into things that are universal," he once explained).

Seinfeld, who says he never bought a joke in his life, also avoids the tricks and shortcuts some comics use, such as profanity, to squeeze laughs out of unfunny routines.

Unlike his friends Jay Leno and David Letterman, Seinfeld mostly stays away from political and topical humor in his stand-up routines in favor of timeless bits he can hone and refine over the course of months—or years.

A 1977 pilot, *Celebrity Cabaret*, featured a twenty-two-year-old Jerry working a room with his stand-up routine. The tape, unearthed by the tabloid show *Hard Copy*, was described by the show's correspondent as "embarrassing." But a closer examination reveals a diamond in the rough. Lurking behind the bell-bottom black suit and wide, unbuttoned shirt collar (which were in style at the time), large glasses, and heavy Lawn Guyland accent were shades of his future success. One routine he performed was the "bumper car" bit, in which Jerry described the "helpless father-and-son team" trying to pilot a broken bumper car at an amusement park. The bit, cleaned and polished to perfection, actually showed up twenty-five years later in the opening monologue of "The Subway" and even in his book, *Sein-Language*.

"He had a nickname among his peers in those days, of Dr. Comedy," recalled Lucien Hold, owner of the Comedy Strip, in a television interview. "That was his nickname, because there was a belief that Jerry could fix any bit."

Seinfeld had a brief encounter with TV in 1980–81, playing Frankie, a

A Stand-Up and His Feet

Jerry once joked that the Ottoman Empire was a civilization based on putting one's feet up, but offstage the comic takes his feet pretty seriously. In fact, he interrupted his busy schedule in late 1994 to fly all the way to the Pacific Northwest for a pair of custom-made corrective foot supports to realign lax joints in his feet.

The lab, Northwest Podiatric Laboratory, Inc., typically fills orders for podiatrists only, not ordinary patients. But Seinfeld insisted on a personal consultation in order to get a good fit, said the lab's marketing director, Ruth Kupp. Kupp got credit for the pickup at Vancouver, B.C., International Airport and drove the star to tiny Blaine, Washington, where the lab is located.

"He's a funny guy, but he's very serious about his feet," Kupp told the *Bellingham Herald*. Kupp said Seinfeld toured the facility and spared the jokes except to say, "Podiatry is funny, and believe me, I'm in the position to know what is funny."

A day later, Seinfeld flew home with his new orthotic devices.

While Jerry's collection of mint-condition sneakers is the stuff of legend, neither sneakers nor shoes cause the problem, said podiatrist and lab co-owner Chris Smith. Age is the culprit: symptoms arise when people hit forty or forty-five.

Because the lab is not insured to provide direct care to patients, the lab was not allowed to charge Seinfeld for the work. Instead, the staff suggested Seinfeld make a donation to the Blaine Boys and Girls Club in lieu of payment. A short while later Seinfeld sent the organization $5,000.

While there's no doubt Jerry is a generous guy, perhaps he felt just a tinge guilty for saying on his show that podiatrists were not real doctors and that "anyone can get into podiatry school" ("The Conversion").

Maybe Jerry began to see things like George Costanza, who said in "The Cheever Letters," "I have tremendous respect for people who work with feet . . . I mean, to dedicate yourself to the foot—you're toiling in virtual anonymity."

messenger, on three episodes of *Benson*, but was unceremoniously written out of the show. He quickly resumed his busy schedule, disenchanted with the television business.

But in 1988 Jerry returned, this time on his own terms. With the help of Larry David, he parlayed his stage persona into a TV special, *The Seinfeld Chronicles*, which aired in 1989 and would become *Seinfeld* a year later. The somewhat autobiographical sitcom, which follows Jerry and his friends through life, became as hard to describe or explain as his act.

"I never thought that I had the kind of style that could be the tremendous, huge success that I am now," he said with a smile on *Entertainment Tonight*. "You know, 'cause I was always kind of low key. But see, I found a thing, see? What I've developed here is reality. And in the context of reality, the low-key approach actually works."

As the only non-actor in a cast of stage and TV veterans, Jerry was understandably nervous about stretching himself too far for the TV-Jerry persona. Early episodes feature his slow, methodical delivery. He stayed away from romantic scenes (and thus handed Jason the beautiful young actresses) and rarely became emotional.

"There are many things I'm embarrassed to do [on the show]," he confessed in 1993, "usually something with a woman. I go to great lengths to keep myself from feeling at all awkward—because I hate it. Comedians are generally very self-conscious people."

In his first effort ("The Seinfeld Chronicles"), Jerry the actor is stiff—but the stand-up segments show the comedian in his element: relaxed, confident, and rolling out some of the best material in his carefully honed repertoire. The next few seasons would show demonstrable improvement in his acting.

Ironically, it was around the time of the 1992–93 season, when the TV Jerry fretted he couldn't act (his exact words in "The Pilot" were "I stink! I don't know what I'm doing!") that Jerry's acting became much better. No longer was he afraid to shout, get physical, kiss women, or go over the top, as his hero Adam West did in *Batman*. He began winning awards for the role. Still, said David, "We try to keep Jerry and Jerry as close as we can. We don't want him to do too much acting."

Although Jerry is close to the character he plays on television, it's not an identical match. When asked if his real apartment was like his TV domain, he joked, "I have a front wall on my apartment."

Seinfeld fans constantly ask the stars and writers what has become of their favorite recurring characters. When the show was honored at the Museum of Television and Radio's ninth annual Television Festival in Los Angeles, Seinfeld responded to such inquiries by reminding the crowd, "It's actually a fictional show—it's not real."

Crossing from comedian to actor is a smaller leap than going the other way, Seinfeld said. He has an easier time delivering his lines than, say, Jason Alexander does warming up the *Seinfeld* studio audience with his stand-up act. "Stand-up is a very specific craft, not unlike playing the saxophone," Seinfeld explained. "If you don't know how, forget it. Acting is like riding a bicycle. You may not compete in the Olympics, but you can keep the pedals going."

Despite the busy schedule and the success, those close to Jerry say he has prepared himself well. These days, he says, what you see is what you get. "I found an acceptable image that was really pretty much me, and that's how I've done everything," he told *Playboy*. "That's why I was able to do the show and why I've succeeded as a comedian."

"Onstage or off, he's never in character, or 'on,' " said *Seinfeld* writer-producer Larry Charles. "He's just him."

In fact, he has become accustomed to encounters with the public on his frequent Manhattan strolls, even if people do act a little too familiar. "When I get dressed in the morning, I'm going out to do a show," he told an interviewer. "You know, I go to the supermarket, and I kind of think about how I look, which I didn't before."

"Jerry as a person is so together," said comedian Carol Leifer, Jerry's ex-girlfriend and a *Seinfeld* writer-producer. "For someone who's never been in therapy, he's amazingly together. It's weird. Because, when he does his stand-up tour, it's like being with a Beatle, people banging on the limo and leaving gifts, but it rolls off his back."

"I had a good feeling about him as soon as I met him," remembered Julia Louis-Dreyfus. "He was exactly where he should be as a levelheaded person. I think the appeal of Jerry Seinfeld is that people watch him and feel like 'Oh yeah, that guy is just like my friend.' "

Larry Miller, the stand-up comic and actor, agreed: "Guys think he's fun to hang out with, and women say they'd love to go out with him."

Louis-Dreyfus said, "He's playing the character Jerry Seinfeld with such aplomb that everybody believes that's really him and feels as if they know him." However, she was quick to make the distinction: "Real Jerry's a very serious guy with a hit television show—and he works hard at it."

Seinfeld is definitely "hands on" when it comes to the show. In addition to starring, he rewrites every script with Larry David, directs some segments, and even supervised the editing of the first 108 episodes—chopping sixty seconds from each show to accommodate the stations that show *Seinfeld* reruns in syndication. "The hardest thing is constantly switching jobs," he once explained. "My personality type is to focus in on one thing, like a laser beam."

He has likened the work schedule to making a round-the-world submarine trip. "You're in there, they seal the hatch, you submerge—and that's all you know for months and months," he said.

Between seasons, Jerry usually makes minitours of the country, playing to sold-out theaters. When he has time, he spends it in his Manhattan "fortress of solitude" or in the Hamptons, the Long Island beach resort of the rich and famous—and those who wish to be. His only real vacation—the first in fourteen years—came in 1993, when he went to Europe with pal Mario Joyner (his right-hand man and comedy-show opener) to hang around Paris and tour the Stuttgart, Germany, fac-

A playful Jerry when he was dividing his love between Shoshanna and the stage. (Vinnie Zuffante/Star File)

tory that built his eight Porsches. He even had to turn down an invitation to appear on Bob Hope's ninetieth-birthday special, featuring Jay Leno, Roseanne, and Johnny Carson.

"You just have to sacrifice what most people would think of as the great fun of being a star: going to premieres and going out to clubs, the social life, the tennis, what everybody would imagine," said Seinfeld. "I don't do any of those things."

"I just spend all my time with the show. That's my whole life. It's not an easy way of living, but it's worth it to have this opportunity. I don't indulge in the fruit of it. Am I missing something? Probably. But more important to me is the health of the project."

"The project," as he calls it, is now seen all over the world, making *Seinfeld* a global phenomenon. "This isn't comedy," Jerry realized in 1992. "It's about suddenly being hot. I've gone from being a comedian who made it to being a guy from a television show."

He has been on the covers of dozens of magazines, including *Rolling Stone* (once by himself, once with the cast), *GQ*, *US* (with Julia Louis-Dreyfus), *Esquire*, *TV Guide*, *Playboy*, and even *Automobile* (he interviewed the designers of a prototype new Volkswagen Beetle).

He has been one of the most in-demand guests on the late-night shows of his friends David Letterman and Jay Leno (a total of over fifty appearances). He even popped up on the fictitious *Larry Sanders Show*, hosted by pal Gary Shandling. In addition to special projects—he hosted a *Spy* magazine special, *Spy TV: How to be Famous* and Showtime's *Aspen Comedy Festival*—he became the national spokesperson for American Express in 1992.

"This has really gotten out of hand," Jerry told the world in his Barbara

Meet Jerry Seinfeld

Walters interview. "People are interested in me now way beyond what is appropriate.

"It's like being on a Ferris wheel," he explained. "This is the top of the wheel. I am right now at the top of the Ferris wheel— and I know what's coming.

"For 98 percent of my career, I was completely at the wheel," he told *Playboy*. "All my perfor-mances, my level, my workload—it was all under control. Now, I'm just hanging on to this thing. My career has now developed a life and a power of its own, and I am just a passenger."

There has been some backlash. Not long after he hosted the *Spy* show, the magazine turned on Seinfeld, naming him number one on the "Spy 100" annual catalog of the year's worst people, places, and things—ranting about Jerry's TV show and personal life. Comedian Bob Goldthwait began wear-ing a T-shirt with the home-made inscription "Kill Seinfeld." "I don't really mean kill him," Goldthwait later said. "It's just how I get out of conversations with yuppies."

Shoshanna-Gate

Jerry's most controversial move was dating a high school senior, Shoshanna Lonstein, in May 1993. CRADLE-SNATCHER, blared the headline of the June 15,

---

Maybe It Was Ocean

Romance writer Judith Krantz once told cable's *Lifetime Magazine* that Jerry is the sexiest man alive.

"I feel that a woman would have a great deal of fun in bed with Jerry," she said. "He looks as if he smells good, too . . . To look as if you smell good on television is an art."

Jerry and Shoshanna wait on deck before he films a scene in "The Understudy." (Vinnie Zuffante/Star File)

1993, *Star*, typical of the tabloid attention. "Seinfeld, 39, flips for high school girl, 17."

That year, Jerry lost his patience with radio talker Howard Stern over comments about the relationship. During an appearance in Atlantic City, Jerry called Stern a "funny jerk" and an "amusing idiot," according to a listener who phoned Stern. Seinfeld appeared on Stern's show and explained it was all in good nature and that the "amusing idiot" crack was a compliment, kind of like comparing him to the Three Stooges, Cheech and Chong, and first brother Roger Clinton.

At that point Jerry said he and Shoshanna had broken up. But they would eventually get back together. The relationship with Stern, however, was over. The final straw came in 1993, during Stern's New Year's Eve pay-per-view special. In addition to a raunchy beauty pageant, the show lampooned Jerry with a musical number featuring Janis Ian singing a parody of her song

"At Seventeen" (a reference to the age Shoshanna was when she met Jerry), complete with an accompanying video of Jerry and Shoshanna lookalikes.

While there are undoubtedly some people left who are shocked to see a showbiz star dating someone half his age, much of the resentment seemed to spring from envy. After all, *Seinfeld* was living a life many can only dream of. "The main reason I get on Jerry so much is that I'm jealous of him," Stern wrote in his bestselling book, *Private Parts*, as if to justify his tormenting of the comedian. As for the twenty-one-year age difference between Jerry and Shoshanna, Stern writes: "How immoral! How wrong! God, how I wish I were doing it."

Although he initially downplayed the seriousness of the relationship, the pair became closer over the following two years, despite some reported breakups and reunions. Seinfeld even visited her on the campus of George Washington University. She later transferred to UCLA to be closer to him.

Perhaps most perplexing was Jerry's reaction to the tabloids: he had none. Jerry refused to stand up to them or to dodge them. "I don't really see the tabloids," he told *Entertainment Weekly*'s Bruce Fretts. "It doesn't bother me. It's all part of being a full-service entertainer."

On occasions, he and Shoshanna played to cameras, alternately smooching or staging a fight. But on the whole, his attitude was to ignore them, and the strategy seemed to work. "Everybody was saying, 'I don't see anything wrong with it. If they like each other . . . ,'" Seinfeld recalled. "My manager couldn't believe it. He said I'm bulletproof even in the tabloids. They had every chance really to stick the knife in and they didn't do it. They could have said anything: I'm taking advantage of her, she doesn't know

Jerry and the "C" Word

"We're pathetic!" Jerry once said to George over a cup of coffee. "Why can't I be normal? It would be nice to care about somebody." While that realization prompted George to propose to Susan in "The Engagement," the real Jerry Seinfeld may not be ready.

"I'd like to settle down," Seinfeld once said. "But for me the fun factor is essential in a mate. That ability to be kidlike, to be a playmate, I have yet to find in a woman. I find it, but not to the extent you build a life on it."

Jerry, a perpetual dater, actually had a brush with marriage once. It was 1984 and he was engaged to a hotel manager he met only a month earlier. But Jerry, then thirty, broke it off within a few months. He then dated a Los Angeles–based publicist off and on between 1986 and 1991. He then began dating a number of top models, including Vendela and Tawny Kitaen.

"I like what's good," said Jerry, when asked about his criteria for women. "Whatever is good, I like that. Good-looking? Yeah. Smart? Yeah, that's good. Sexy? Good."

"I tend not to like ugly, dumb, hostile women," he told Barbara Walters, "I find them less attractive, frankly."

"Even Superman can't make a commitment," he rationalized. "Why give me a hard time? If he, with all his powers, can't get it together, why should I be able to?"

However, any potential Mrs. Seinfeld should be aware of her competition. Jerry's main relationship in life is with the audience.

"That's the love affair that has kept me going all this time," he told *Dateline*'s Jane Pauley. "It's very intense, you know, when people laugh at something you like, and they agree with you. There's a moment there that's truly romantic."

what's going on, her parents are upset, my mother wanted to disown me. They could have made up anything."

While most of the controversy surrounded the age difference, Seinfeld is not the first Hollywood star to date someone half his age. Nor will he be the last.

"[I]t's still hard for me to believe that anyone gives a damn who the hell I go out with or what I do," he once said. Seinfeld and Shoshanna called it quits in early 1997, seemingly putting a final chapter to their on-again-off-again romance. Some said she was pushing for a marriage commitment to coincide with her graduation from UCLA. But according to a Seinfeld friend quoted in the *New York Post*, "There was no nasty scene. They both knew it was time for a break."

Managing Success

By 1994, the focus was back on Jerry's career and his TV show—and whether he would still do it. When Jerry fueled rumors that he was preparing to pull the plug on the show, NBC took notice. Warren Littlefield, president of NBC entertainment, dressed up like a waiter and served the cast bagels and juice at a script reading.

"I think that even the best TV series has a healthy life of five to eight years," Jerry once pontificated. "You can go longer, based on your ratings and all, but that's just milking it."

Working just for the money was well behind Seinfeld. In addition to his salary—some $800,000 per episode, which NBC matched the first time an episode is rerun—Jerry was also getting a sizable chunk of the $200 million to $300 million in syndication fees. He pulled in a reported $1.5 million advance from his million-selling *SeinLanguage*, plus more than $1 million from his American Express commercials.

TV Guide had named Seinfeld one of TV's Most Powerful Stars—he came in fifth, between Roseanne (fourth) and Barbara Walters/Diane Sawyer (tied for sixth)—for his 30-million-plus demographically desirable TV viewers and the show's advertiser price tag: $390,000 for thirty seconds.

Jerry has so far resisted the temptation to shoot quickie movies in his off time like other sitcom stars, mostly because he feels there are too many factors that go into moviemaking. Onstage, he says, a comedian can control just about everything about his performance. While he does have a film deal with Castle Rock (the studio which produces his television show), Seinfeld is nowhere close to starting the project. When he does, however, he insists it will be done the same way he does his show—on his terms, with him calling the shots.

"Look at those people from *Saturday Night Live*, going into those dumb movies," Seinfeld told *GQ*. "You want to say to them, 'What happened to what you were trying to do?' "

In the meantime, the comedian still enjoyed stand-up, often showing up at old haunts like New York's Catch A Rising Star for an unscheduled set—either to test new material or just work out some favorite routines in front of a live crowd.

"Being up there alone, exposed. You can't cheat, can't fool anyone," he explained. "You've either done the work—or everyone knows you haven't. It's the ultimate personality stress test."

As Jerry told comedian Alan King on the Comedy Central network, he simply enjoys "the purity, the simplicity" of stand-up. "If you get it right, it's perfect entertainment," Seinfeld said.

"Oh, I love TV, too," he told another interviewer, "but I'll never do another TV show. I can't imagine trying to top what we've got. I'd like to do a movie. But I'll always come back to stand-up."

"I want them to know that comedy is my life's work, that a lot of work has gone into this," he explained. "It isn't something cobbled together after the show became a hit in order to make some extra money. It's not Suzanne Somers going on tour in Las Vegas after *Three's Company*—nothing against Suzanne Somers."

He has always been indefinite about ending the show. He never expected it to catch on in the first place. When it did, he tossed out a figure of "five years." Now he leaves it up in the air.

"I can guarantee you we won't do ten [seasons]," he stated in *Playboy*. "I don't want to be in people's faces. This show is going to be off way sooner than anyone would believe."

"It's like an act," he said of the series in an interview with *Dateline*. "It has flow, a peak, and a time. And I always get off early. It's better. I don't like restaurants that serve a lot of food. When people tell me 'the portions are tremendous,' that doesn't appeal to me. Sheer volume is not attractive to me. And same goes for the number of episodes that we do. I want to do enough shows that people can say, 'You know, every one was good.' "

Dr. J

"All right, all right, just let me tell jokes to strangers in nightclubs for eighteen years, and I'm sure they'll make me a doctor!"

It may not have been as simple as Jerry Seinfeld described it to a Queens College commencement audience in the spring of 1994, but nevertheless, he received an honorary doctorate from his alma mater amid a media frenzy the

Jerry's John Hancock

Although Jerry Seinfeld is a consistent top ten in the ratings, his autograph etiquette leaves a lot to be desired—so says Cindy Starr, a columnist for *Autograph Collector* magazine. Based on her own experiences and discussions with autograph collectors, Starr placed Jerry on the list of 1995's 10 Worst Autograph Signers. Jerry ranked seventh on the list, better than Macaulay Culkin, Bruce Willis, Anna Paquin, Kevin Costner, Mel Gibson, and the worst signer of the year, The Artist Formerly Known As Prince.

"Usually, when approached, [Jerry] gets a pained look on his face, refuses nastily and sometimes even finishes off the exchange with a 'get lost,' " Starr says. "What a sweetheart, huh?" For making the list, Starr bestowed on Jerry the uncoveted "Platinum Prune Award."

Jerry's John Hancock is worth anywhere from $40 to $95, according to dealers; a picture signed by the cast fetches up to $200.

To be fair, we've heard stories to the contrary. And those lucky people who have found Jerry willing to sign autographs offer these tips:

1. Be Female
2. Be Attractive
3. Be Alone

school had never seen before. (Seinfeld, who studied theater arts and mass communications, graduated in 1976.)

The faculty senate nominated the comic earlier in 1994 for an honorary doctorate, and the plan was approved by the City University of New York trustees provided that Seinfeld pick up the diploma in person. And even though he is perhaps the school's most visible alumnus, Seinfeld was not a shoe-in for the award, which recognizes "someone who has achieved national distinction in some area of education at Queens College." Several members of the faculty senate felt Seinfeld didn't measure up to previous recipients, who include Aaron Copland, Jonas Salk, Marvin Hamlisch, Toni Morrison, and Dizzy Gillespie.

"Giving a serious degree to a comedian is not a normal thing," philosophy professor John Lange told the school paper, the *QC Quad*. "If [Seinfeld] wasn't a graduate, he never would have been considered."

Library studies professor Harry Kibirage told the paper Seinfeld has given "no major contributions to intellectual development" and "no serious lasting, reach-out commitments . . . He's an entertainer. So is Madonna."

However, the academic senate believed Seinfeld merited the award and passed a resolution that stated: "[Seinfeld] has gained national stature as a theatrical, club, and TV star of the highest magnitude. He is also a bestselling author. He has built his early education in Theater and Communications at Queens College and is proud of his association with the college . . . He is a performer with the genius for transforming the ordinary details of life into extraordinary comedy."

"I'm very glad that Seinfeld is coming back to Queens College," said Forbes Hill, one of Jerry's former professors. "He clearly has given the college a great amount of publicity and has served as a Queens College booster and supporter."

Students were also thrilled about a homecoming for Seinfeld, who was already something of a phenomenon on campus. When he wore school colors (a cap in "The Barber" and a T-shirt in "The Mango"), the bookstore could not keep them in stock. A couple of years later, he was still true to his school, wearing a white Queens College tee in "The Pool Guy."

Queens Borough President Claire Shulman congratulates Jerry on his honorary doctorate, eighteen years after he left Queens College. (Office of the Queens Borough President)

The college even used the publicity in a recruiting campaign. A brochure opened with the headline: "What do Jerry Seinfeld, Paul Simon, Charles Wang [CEO, Computer Associates], and Jill Barad [president, Mattel Toys] have in common? They all graduated from Queens College."

The student paper praised the homecoming as "a public relations masterstroke and a lucrative donation opportunity."

As he made his way across the quadrangle toward the podium, the comedian ignored questions from the flock of reporters who addressed him as "Dr. Seinfeld," saving his remarks for the audience.

"I spent several wonderful years here at Queens College," Seinfeld told the crowd, which included mom Betty and sister Carolyn and a horde of photographers. "I would say that the best parking spot I ever got was in my junior year. It was right out here on Kissena Boulevard near Melbourne [Avenue]. I didn't even have to parallel. I pulled right in. It was a beautiful spot. I generally didn't even attempt to park on this side of the expressway."

Seinfeld seemed almost surprised at the warm reception.

"I tell you with the job market you're facing, you're a terrific audience," he quipped.

"It was a little more casual than I had hoped," said spokesperson Ron Cannava. "We hoped he would have taken the opportunity to say more." Nevertheless, Jerry's two-minute address gave the school more media attention than anyone could remember and gave the 3,300 graduates and their 10,000 guests a few laughs.

"He's a doctor. He made it," his mother was heard saying before taking the family out for milkshakes.

Seinfeld's faculty adviser, Edward Greenberg, recalled in an interview spending thirty minutes each week with his student, advising him what material was going to work, and what would not. "We spent the time sharpening his tools," recalled Greenberg, who has directed many comics, including Bob Hope. "He told me his new jokes and I gave him my opinion."

Greenberg, who remembered Jerry as "hard-working," told the *Quad*,

Superman vs. "Seinfeld-man"

In the bizarre world of *Seinfeld*, Jerry often finds himself the outsider looking in . . . not unlike his hero, Superman. Wait a second . . .

Superman . . .

Lives in Metropolis.
Hides his secret identity from villains.
Battles the evil forces of Lex Luthor.
Is faster than a speeding bullet.

Can't withstand exposure to Kryptonite.

Encounters weird creatures from the Cosmos.

"Seinfeld-man" . . .

Lives in metropolitan New York.
Hides his "ugly side" from girlfriends.
Battles the evil forces of Newman.
Is faster than a high school rival (albeit by cheating).
Can't withstand exposure to Kramer's Jockey shorts.
Lives next door to a weird creature named Cosmo.

"He is a nice young man, actually very much like the character he portrays on television."

No word on when some of the school's other funny alumni—including Fran Drescher and Joy Behar—will get their honorary degrees. "Queens College breeds comedy, because you have to have a sense of humor to cope on this campus," explained Asaf Ronen, a member of the school's improv group, Newmyn's Nose. "Have you ever dealt with the registrar?"

Seinfeld seemed impressed with himself for weeks after the ceremony. "I'm a doctor now," he quipped in *Esquire.* "And the interesting thing is, I'm a cardiologist. I was completely unprepared for that when they gave me the degree. I said, 'I really don't know anything about cardiology.' They said, 'That's okay. Just do what you know.' "

Jerry Seinfeld: In His Own Words

On casting Elaine: "I was looking for the kind of woman that I'm looking for in life, the kind of woman with a certain strength in character through humor."

On cereal: "It was the first thing I could make when I was a kid. I was proud of it. I love milk."

On finding a joke: "The joke is the fleck of gold after going through a ton of rock . . . The whole world is rock. I've found this little lump of gold—my comedy material—and I've made it into an act."

On Jason Alexander: "I don't think he realizes how much I secretly look up to him. In some ways, he's like a younger big brother to me."

On stand-up comedy: "The funny thing about being a comedian is, you have to have this great love for humanity on a mass level. Because that's why you work so hard to do something good for people you don't even know—and yet still manage to absolutely hate every single individual that you come in contact with."

On Michael Richards: "People know what you show them. He shows me that he is a perfectionist. That much I know."

On age: "Most comedians think of their ages as the number of years they've been performing."

On keeping the show going: "It's a little like watching the N.B.A. You're amazed that they keep doing those things, but they do. I'm still amazed we're able to do it."

On exposure: "There are still a few places where I am not—and I don't like it. I don't like it one bit!"

On money: "One of the most fun things is not having to worry about money, to not have to waste mental time thinking about it. That's nicer than almost anything you can buy with it."

On his TV career: "[*Seinfeld*] is not my job. I'm a comedian. This is just something I was fortunate enough to get to do. My job is to write jokes, go to Milwaukee, and tell them."

On sexual politics: "Well, I've always said that women have more power than men. We live in a vagocracy."

On picking up women: "I've always employed the tractor-beam system of female attraction. I try and lock 'em in on the beam, like in *Star Trek*, and then pull them in."

On his sexual fantasy: "I think to have sex with Madonna would be really fun. Because I'd love to just hitch up my pants afterward and say, 'I'll bet you thought that was really something else, huh?' "

Meet Jason Alexander

By the time Jason Alexander got to Boston University in the late 1970s, he was well on his way to fulfilling his dream of becoming an actor. He had performed in school shows, commercials (since the age of fourteen), community theater, and a television pilot for PBS.

But in 1979, when he was cast in a feature film, *The Burning*, he left Boston—where he had won a drama scholarship—for a career in New York. *The Burning*, a horror flick in the *Friday the 13th* genre, never won any Academy Awards. But it sent Alexander to New York with a movie under his belt and a wide-open future. He took a job in a casting agent's office, where he would meet his future wife, an actress and writer named Daena Title.

Responding to an open call, Title walked into Alexander's office for an audition. Smitten at first sight, Alexander scheduled her for a second reading. A relationship developed, then flourished, and two years later he took her to Times Square, where a message flashed on a one-hundred-foot-high electronic billboard: "Daena, I love you. Please marry me. Forever, Jason."

While the line between *Seinfeld*'s cast and characters is a thin one, Alexander says he is not nutty George Costanza—but he could have been.

"I always felt loved, I always had a job, and I didn't have parents who were as wacked-out as [George's]," he once said.

"If my life had not gone as well as it has, I could have been more like George," he said. "The impetus to play him comes from somewhere inside me."

Born Jay Scott Greenspan on September 23, 1959, in Newark, New Jersey, Alexander had a "disgustingly normal" childhood in Maplewood and nearby Livingston with his father, a manager at a manufacturing plant, and his mother, a nurse, and two half-siblings. As with many funny people, Alexander developed his performing skills at an early age—the first grade—as a shield to protect himself from kids who taunted him about his weight problem.

"I was a very heavy and, in retrospect, kind of a scared little kid," Alexander recalled. "I was constantly being harassed . . . I was always nervous that I was going to be abused by the other kids.

Between *Seinfeld, Duckman,* and a busy movie schedule, Jason somehow manages to attend an occasional movie premiere with wife Daena Title. (Vinnie Zuffante/Star File)

"I figured out the golden rule of comedy: If you make the other kids laugh, they won't make fun of you. They may even like you," he told a group of kids at his alma mater. "So I became as funny as I could be by memorizing every movie script, TV show, and comedy album that I could."

Alexander listened to comedy albums by people like Bill Cosby, Bob Newhart, and George Carlin and would learn their routines. "Half the time I didn't even know what I was saying," he recalled. "But I instinctively knew that if the kids were laughing, they couldn't hurt me. I never performed in class, because I was secure there. I'd do it in playgrounds and wherever I felt when I wasn't safe."

"Performing was my defense," he told *TV Guide*, "and then it became sort of my fist . . . it gave me, for the first time in my life, power."

Alexander's early musical influences—he was fond of soundtracks such as *The Fantasticks*—also had a lasting influence. By the time he was five, Alexander says he could sing the scores of two dozen shows.

It was at his bar mitzvah, where he conducted a lengthy ceremony, that Alexander thought, "I might really like to be a performer."

His role model then (and now) was William Shatner, of *Star Trek* fame. "I became an actor because of Shatner," he explained. "Everywhere I went as a kid, I was doing the best Shatner you've ever seen." Years later, Alexander even wanted a guest spot in *Star Trek: The Next Generation*, said the show's executive producer, Rick Berman. (Had it not gone off the air, he probably would have gotten to walk the hallowed decks of the *Enterprise*.)

When he was sixteen, Alexander joined a local theater group called the Pushcart Players, which made a pilot for PBS—*The Pushcart Players: Feelings and Friends*. Alexander, as luck would have it, became the star when he filled in for one of the lead actors who had taken ill.

High school drama coach Robert Lampf remembers meeting the aspiring actor in 1974: "Within ten minutes I was telling anyone who'd listen: This kid was born to be onstage. This kid is going to make it."

"He had an aura, a presence, an ability to move people emotionally," Lampf recalled. "[He] had the lead in every high school play, and he was the star of every show. Yet he was totally unspoiled and unpretentious."

Lampf said Alexander brought down the house at Livingston High School's Annual Talent Night when he asked the rarely seen principal, "Excuse me, who are you?"

Alexander received a drama scholarship to Boston University, and later the prestigious Harold C. Case Award for scholarship and service. At Boston he refined his stage skills (and practiced magic in Boston Common for spare change), but he left BU when feature film work—*The Burning*—called, and teamed him with another unknown bound for greatness, Holly Hunter.

At twenty, known professionally as Jason Alexander (although he never officially changed his name), he landed a part in *Merrily We Roll Along* (he jokes it became a legend as the first Stephen Sondheim flop) and began a steady succession of parts on Broadway, including *Broadway Bound*, *The Rink*, and *Jerome Robbins' Broadway*, and Off-Broadway, in *Personals*, *Forbidden Broadway*, and *Stop the World, I Want to Get Off*. Later, he portrayed Harry Truman in the one-man play *Give 'Em Hell Harry* in Los Angeles.

Yet there were obstacles along the way. Alexander's physical appearance relegated him to boisterous, funny roles as opposed to the serious leads for which he was better suited emotionally. He often summarizes his struggle by comparing his dream role, Hamlet, with the role casting directors had in mind: Falstaff. "It took a lot to embrace the fact that I could be a Falstaff who had the heart of a Hamlet," he explained.

For an extroverted (some say natural) performer, another obstacle seems surprising: severe stage fright. His first night on Broadway, in *Merrily We Roll Along*, was almost catastrophic. "When the curtain went up, I thought I was going to keel over," he told a reporter. "I didn't want to tell anybody, because I thought I'd be fired. And the fear of it happening again is what made it happen again and again."

He recalled that in Neil Simon's *Broadway Bound*, his character had to sleep onstage for 10 minutes. "I had to lie still, and I was petrified," he told *Parade* magazine. "My hand would dig into the bed, and sweat poured off me. I was in a blind panic." (George paid tribute to Jason's past by wearing a *Broadway Bound* T-shirt in "The Alternate Side.")

By 1989, when he played the narrator in *Jerome Robbins' Broadway* (doing lines he had written), Alexander overcame his anxiety with professional help and his own mantra: "Strength. Courage. Conviction. Joy." That year he won the Tony, Outer Critics, and Drama Desk awards for Best Actor in a Musical.

In 1995, he returned to his roots in an ABC remake of the musical *Bye Bye Birdie*, starring with Vanessa Williams and Tyne Daly. Alexander floored critics with his singing and dancing (*Newsweek* said he had the grace of Gene Kelly).

Although he insists he never went looking for television parts, "TV found me." His TV credits included NBC's miniseries *Favorite Son*, the TV movies *Rockabye* and *Senior Trip*, a short-lived series, *Everything's Relative*, and the hospital sitcom, *E/R* (*not* the top-rated NBC drama *ER*). Couch potatoes have probably seen Alexander hundreds more times pitching McDonald's McD.L.T. sandwiches (in an elaborate song-and-dance number) or in a

Southern police station calling home for bail money ("Is there any way you could send the money . . . today?") for Western Union, or in dozens more commercials.

Just as TV found Alexander, so did Jerry Seinfeld and Larry David when they were casting the *Seinfeld* special for NBC. Seinfeld recalled that the pair looked at Alexander's audition tape and knew they had their George.

"He was so exactly what we had in mind," Seinfeld said, "that we never considered another actor."

Alexander's acting experience even helped him get women—on the show, that is. "For the first three seasons, Jerry was uncomfortable being an actor," Alexander explained. "He didn't want to do anything he didn't feel comfortable doing, like getting angry or having a romantic scene. At that point, they didn't feel Kramer could be a secret weapon to women. So the only guy left was me. I got thrown all of Jerry's refuse."

So how does it feel to be a part of the hit show?

"It's great, it's fun," he said, "but it doesn't mean you're made for life, or that you're an important person or a better person."

Still, Alexander is removed from the character for which he has won several awards. "He is exactly the opposite of the character," David said. "He's confident, he has a lot of patience, and he always maintains a calm demeanor."

"Anybody running up to me to meet George is in trouble," Alexander explained. "Emotionally, I understand him. I don't know that I am him, but I understand him."

One would think that Alexander would be doomed to George Costanza–type roles for years. But while *Seinfeld* ruled the airwaves, Alexander slipped convincingly in and out of movie roles by surrendering his Costanza spectacles (they're just part of the costume), dabbing on some makeup, and perhaps putting on a wig or mustache. Alexander has none of the George persona in a diverse crop of movies from the late 1980s through the mid-1990s, including *I Don't Buy Kisses Anymore, White Palace, The Mosquito Coast, Brighton Beach Memoirs, Blankman, Jacob's Ladder, Coneheads, North, The Paper*, and *Dunston Checks In*.

Alexander also provides the voice of the libidinous, animated cartoon gumshoe in the USA Network's *Duckman*. "[Duckman] is a very lowbrow, sexually oriented angry duck detective," Alexander said on *Live With Regis and Kathie Lee*. Duckman's signature line is, "What the hell are *you* staring at?!?"

"A lot of actors—and very good actors—are basically who they are in their performances," he said. "I actively make a decision to make each character as different as I can. I always got off on being chameleonlike."

Alexander even poked fun at the world of independent filmmaking in the Academy Award–nominated short *Down on the Waterfront*, in which he starred with Edward Asner.

In one of his best-remembered roles, the low-life lawyer friend of Richard Gere's character in *Pretty Woman*, Alexander's character sexually assaults Julia Roberts's character. "I was the scumball of the United States," he said. "I struck Julia Roberts."

Making matters worse was that Roberts, then twenty and virtually unknown, had no formal stage-fighting experience. So it was Alexander, ironically, who got roughed up. "When it came time to shoot the rape scene, it was hell," he said in 1993, when he returned to Boston University for a special School for the Arts Alumni Award. "Here's a girl who doesn't know stage

On the Serious Side

Taking a humorous approach to a serious problem, the Centers for Disease Control and Prevention tapped Jason Alexander in 1994 to do a thirty-second radio spot for America Responds to AIDS. The national campaign, which also featured other actors (Martin Lawrence read a similar script) as well as TV ads, was denounced by some conservatives and clerics as lewd.

Title: "Mic"
Agency: Ogilvy & Mather South

JASON ALEXANDER: Suppose my voice were HIV, and listening could infect you. You wouldn't listen. You'd change the station or turn off the radio. Am I right? Buuuut . . . if I took a latex condom and put it on this microphone . . . (muffled sounds). You couldn't hear me. Could you? So you were protected from HIV. That's exactly what latex condoms do. So remember, sex without a latex condom isn't always safe. Listening to me, on the other hand, well . . . always safe.

ANNOUNCER: Call 1-800-342-AIDS for a free brochure.

---

combat, would bite my hand. I was bruised and battered and I was trying not to upset this actress while doing this scene."

Alexander also hosted *Saturday Night Live* in 1993 (despite warnings about the grueling pace and lackluster material from previous host Jerry and former cast member Julia Louis-Dreyfus), enlivening the show by showcasing his singing and dancing, with nary a mention of *Seinfeld*.

These days, Alexander still keeps to his philosophy: to make the best with what you've got.

"Most people like to laugh," he told a *Hard Copy* interviewer. "But in Hollywood it's hard to find people who look like gods who are funny. They'd rather have a schlemiel like me."

"I never had a good year," he said, typically self-effacing. "I had nine years of orthodontia, and the day the braces came off, the hair started falling out."

His image as an everyman—an everyman fighting the battle of the bulge—won him the lead in a series of successful TV commercials for Rold Gold Fat Free pretzels.

Offscreen, the cerebral Alexander displayed a knack for Broadway musicals and nuclear physics in a 1994 celebrity *Jeopardy!* tournament, besting Marilu Henner and Lou Diamond Phillips and winning $11,800 for his charity, the Anti-Defamation League.

He recently read *A Brief History of Time* by British astrophysicist Stephen Hawking, and as a guest critic for *People* magazine, he planted tongue in cheek. "I felt [Hawking] was speaking to me at my level," he said. "You know, so many people write down to me. I wrote to him and said, 'You didn't say things as clearly as I would,' but he did a very good job."

Alexander still sings whenever he gets the chance. His tribute to the great television theme songs of old on the telecast of the 46th annual primetime Emmy awards blended snippets from three dozen pop culture staples (such as *The Brady Bunch*, *All in the Family*, and *The Flintstones*) and highlighted an otherwise dull awards show. Prior to another singing engagement—a Stephen Sondheim tribute at the Kennedy Center—Alexander and Title were invited to the White House. But in a page out of a *Seinfeld* script, Alexander froze up when it came time to meet President and Mrs. Clinton.

"We get up to the president," he recalled, "and suddenly, I've lost all powers of speech. He smiles, shakes our hands. Hillary smiles. We stand side by side and flash bulbs burst. It's time to move on and I realize I haven't said a word, so I turn to Hillary and say, 'You have a very lovely home here.' What a schmuck! I mean, it's the goddamn White House, and I'm saying 'You have a lovely home'? Then we move on to the vice president. Miraculously, now I'm Mr. Career Diplomat. I'm completely transformed. 'Hello, Mr. Vice President, Mrs. Gore. I'm Jason Alexander, this is my wife, Daena.' And we chat and I think, 'Why couldn't I have woken up two minutes ago?' It was just so George."

Despite the trappings of fame, he remains down-to-earth: "Getting recognized on the street, writing, directing, acting, even meeting the president of the United States, you just can't take it all too seriously. Then again, you definitely can't take it for granted."

For Alexander, the recent addition of a child, Gabriel, has changed his perspective on life. "I've never loved anyone like this before," he said. "He's changed me in so many ways. I've become a more readily emotional person. He makes me more vulnerable."

Alexander said having a son has made him more aware of the world around him. "I need to know what's going on everywhere, because every child is like my kid," he explained. "If something can happen to this kid, it can happen to my kid."

Perhaps it was this new outlook that convinced Alexander to lend his talents to groups like America Responds to AIDS, a nonprofit organization, which launched a TV and radio ad campaign aimed at preventing the spread of HIV. The socially conscious actor also teamed up with TV costar Julia Louis-Dreyfus for two readings of *Bunny Bunny,* a book of transcribed con-

Next Time, He'll Take Her Word for It

Jason Alexander will never forget the first time he met Elizabeth Taylor. It was back on Broadway when he heard a knock on his dressing room door. The voice said it was "Elizabeth Taylor."

"I thought, 'Yeah, right,' " Alexander told *USA Today*. "I throw off the robe, I drop the boxers, and I open the door . . . and it *is* Elizabeth Taylor. She's the only woman other than my wife who's been forced to see [me nude] and is still willing to be in a room with me!"

Alexander and Taylor were "reunited" when they met up in 1993 at a Big Sisters of Los Angeles event honoring Taylor's friend and neighbor, songwriter Carole Bayer Sager. He was wearing pants at the time.

versations between comedy writer Alan Zweibel and the late comic Gilda Radner to benefit the Gilda's Club charity.

Alexander's anxiety about not working has driven him to tackle singing, dancing, and so many diverse acting roles. The next phase for the all-around performer is directing. He helmed a Castle Rock feature film, *For Better or Worse*, in which he also starred.

One recurring fear Alexander has is that *Seinfeld* will go off the air, "no one will hire me, we'll run out of money, and I'll spend my last years wandering around morosely asking, 'Do you remember . . . ?' "

What's worse, he says, is the possibility that he may be doing his *Seinfeld* part so well that audiences will not accept him as anything but the whiny, immature George Costanza.

"It's happened to other people," he told an interviewer. "Think of Carroll O'Connor when he was the star of *All in the Family*—the *Seinfeld* of its day. He was phenomenally good on it, but when the show ended, he became, as far as I can see, a pariah for years, before he ended up on another series.

Why? Because he was Archie Bunker to the world and they wouldn't accept him as anything else. He had to wait a generation for that image to be cleared out of everybody's heads before he could get on with his life. When you're in a show that makes such a strong impression, you never know what'll happen to you next."

"Fear has motivated me to never be in a position where I don't get work because there's something I can't do," he told *Parade*. "If they say, 'Do you sing?' I say 'yes.' If they say, 'Can you dance?' I say 'yes.' I try to stay in the theater. I try to stay in feature films. I'm moving into directing. The idea is to always have enough going for me so that nobody can say 'no' to me forever. I may have trouble believing that the work will always be there, but there's a certain confidence I do have: If you give me a job, I know I can do it. Absolutely."

Jason Alexander: In His Own Words

On Julia Louis-Dreyfus: "Julia is able to be . . . one of the guys and really hold her own, and never lose the fact that she's a very feminine and lovely woman."

On being like George: "You know, I'm sure all the basic paranoia and the neurosis are in there somewhere, but I'm married to a beautiful woman, who thinks I'm adorable, and I have a job. I guess if you took all that away, I could very well be George."

On his confident manner: "I'm one of the more scared people I know. But I cover it with this veneer of absolute calm, almost to the point of being cocky."

On theater: "I love being onstage. The joy was always greater than the fear. But the fear was very real."

On Jerry Seinfeld: "Let me tell you something. If anything happens to Jerry, my life's not worth living! I'm a million and a half in debt right now. I'd take a bullet [for Jerry] in a minute."

On the *Seinfeld* cast: "Of the four of us, I am the least naturally funny in the group. If you put the four of us at a party and said, 'Be lively and entertaining,' you'd gravitate to the other three long before me."

On George Costanza: "I think of George as a fairly good-hearted guy whose biggest downfall is that he doesn't think much of himself. Nebbish is one word that comes to mind. Pathetic is another."

On seeing his childhood idol, William Shatner: "I broke into a huge sweat. I don't know if he knows who I am. I didn't say a word. I figure he's got enough psychos following him. He doesn't need one more."

On Fabio: "What bothers me about guys like that is they can walk into any clothing store, pick up a shirt, put it on, walk out—and it looks great! *That's never happened in my life!*"

On fame: "You know, you can be Joe Schmoe, but if you're on TV for three weeks, people will take your picture."

Meet Julia Louis-Dreyfus

Smart, beautiful, and talented, Julia Louis-Dreyfus grew up with show business in her veins. As a child, she staged plays for friends and neighbors in Bethesda, Maryland, near Washington, D.C., casting herself in the starring roles. Her parents were adamant about not letting her become a professional child actress, so Julia pursued her love of acting as president of the drama club at the Holton-Arms school, an exclusive all-girls high school in Bethesda. While she delighted classmates in school productions, including the comedy *You Can't Take It With You*, some students and teachers found themselves on the receiving end of her vicious comic impersonations off-stage.

A year after she was born on January 13, 1961, in New York City, Louis-Dreyfus's parents were divorced. At the age of eight, she moved to Washington, where she was raised with two half-sisters by her mother, a writer, and her stepfather, a doctor. But she spent summers and school vacations with her father, a businessman-lawyer, and stepmother, a teacher, and their two daughters at their estate in Mount Kisco, New York. She is close with both halves of the family.

After high school, Louis-Dreyfus moved to Illinois, where she studied theater at Northwestern University and worked at both the Practical Theatre improv company, where she was the only female cast member, and the renowned Second City comedy troupe (the company that launched comic greats such as John Belushi, Gilda Radner, and Bill Murray). It was at Northwestern that freshman Louis-Dreyfus, nineteen, met her future husband, the writer/producer/actor Brad Hall, a recent grad who worked with Practical Theatre. In 1982, the summer between her junior and senior year, still working with both troupes, Louis-Dreyfus was approached to join the cast of *Saturday Night Live* after producers caught a special revue performance, *The Practical Theatre's Golden 50th Anniversary Jubilee*. Louis-Dreyfus and Hall, who was also cast, moved to New York City and were married five years later.

While her star was rising, the years she spent on *SNL* were tumultuous. Cast members came and went with great frequency. Julia's tenure—three seasons—was a testament to her versatility.

But Julia faced what has been described as institutional disregard for women from the writers, producers, and even other cast members, who relegated women to fewer skits and smaller roles than their male counterparts, who included Eddie Murphy, Joe Piscopo, and Billy Crystal.

"It was bad there . . . Pret-ty bad . . ." she recalled. "It didn't occur to them to give women certain roles," she said. "In a way, I can understand that a guy writing a sketch is going to be more oriented to men."

Yet complaints to then-producer Dick Ebersol were ineffective. Louis-Dreyfus said she complained "all the time," but "it was not received. Nobody cared. Strange, huh?"

And while Louis-Dreyfus remembers the seasons as "difficult, harrowing, and not even that much fun," she took it as a learning experience: "[I]t taught me about what those experiences are like—and they're rampant in this business.

"It was an extremely political environment," she said, "and I'm not talking about government. Ultimately, I learned that it's not worth it unless you're having a good time."

Years later, she would mention her experiences to Billy Crystal. "He was surprised," Louis-Dreyfus said. "He didn't have any idea." Today, Louis-Dreyfus tactfully declines to trash the show, even in its critical nadir.

"It's like badmouthing your rich uncle who sent you through college," she told columnist Liz Smith. "Maybe he's a creep and he never listened to you and treated other people better than you, but . . . he put you through college."

After *SNL*, Louis-Dreyfus landed the part of Chevy Chase's snooty neighbor in *National Lampoon's Christmas Vacation*. In 1988–89, she appeared in *Day By Day*, an NBC sitcom about a day-care center,

Although she was looking for a leading role, Julia Louis-Dreyfus couldn't pass up the lure of *Seinfeld*'s sassy Elaine character, a role that won her a Golden Globe in 1994. (Jeff Mayer/Star File)

as Eileen Swift, a fast-track stockbroker who hated children. While the show was short-lived, it led to more roles in movies, including *Hannah and Her Sisters*, in which Louis-Dreyfus played Woody Allen's assistant.

It was in the late eighties that she was handed a *Seinfeld* script. The rest is TV history. "Normally I would have hesitated," she said, "because my inclination would have been to get a lead . . . But the writing was truly spectacular."

There was no female lead in the original *Seinfeld* mix. Jerry Seinfeld and Larry David had finished *The Seinfeld Chronicles*, a one-shot NBC special about Jerry, George, and Kramer, which aired in July 1989. But when NBC ordered four more episodes, they pressed for a female character. Jerry recalled that the show "lacked estrogen."

David, who had known Louis-Dreyfus since the early- to mid-'80s *SNL* days, set up a meeting in January 1990 over—what else?—a bowl of cereal. Seinfeld knew he had found his Elaine.

"We had a very vague idea of Elaine," Seinfeld told the *New York Times*. "But once Julia walked in, we knew who Elaine was. We created her together."

Seinfeld said he admired Julia's ability to be "sweet and attractive" while holding her own comedically. "That is an extremely rare quality in show business."

As Elaine Marie Benes, the ex-girlfriend of stand-up comedian Jerry Seinfeld, Louis-Dreyfus adds a refreshing female perspective to the male-dominated cast. Yet the character is more than just a supporting player. Elaine is, above all, an individual, with her own job and active love life.

"It seems a lot of women characters in TV and film are just girlfriends or wisecracking best friends or mothers—appendages of males and not people who stand solidly on their own," Louis-Dreyfus once explained. "I'm happy to play a woman who is not defined only by her relationships to the men on the show," she once explained. "She's an interesting person and not just 'the woman' on the show. It's definitely nice not to have to prove myself as the woman cast member every week. It's nice to be on equal terms with everybody. It's a nice space to be in."

While she says she's no way "nearly as neurotic" as her character, Louis-Dreyfus says Elaine "is very much like myself, times 150. She's a fairly stable, high-strung woman who's independent but a little confused about where she's going."

"Julia is so likable and sweet on one level that we can give her dark things to play, which she makes palatable," explained Larry Charles. "Somehow she makes it acceptable to the audience."

While the writers have been hesitant to exploit Louis-Dreyfus's sheer good looks, her beauty has come into play when the scene calls for a skin-tight leotard. Even George freezes up when he sees a naked "Elaine" mannequin in "The Pie."

In perhaps her sexiest *Seinfeld* performance, "The Tape," Elaine leaves an anonymous sexy message on a tape recorder Jerry uses to record his act. When the three find out it was she who left the message, they all become turned on. Elaine also arouses George when she vamps for Kramer's video camera, pretending to be a porno actress being interviewed about her career.

"I had no idea you were filled with such . . . sexuality," George confesses to her in one scene.

In a more recent episode, "The Gum," Elaine loses a button from her blouse, exposing cleavage and inadvertently teasing Lloyd Braun, an ex-boyfriend who recently suffered a nervous breakdown.

"We rarely touch on this, but there has to be some sexual attraction," said Jason Alexander, "not necessarily from Elaine for the guys, but each of

What a Sweetie

The Sincerely Gourmet Chocolates company named Julia Louis-Dreyfus one of 1995's most romantic women. In a poll conducted by the confection maker, candy buyers and celebs (including romance-novel cover-boy Fabio, rich and famous confidante male Robin Leach, and often-married talk-show host Larry King) said her private life and public work "contributes to the development of romance as one of life's essential elements."

the guys has a thing for her at some point and that gets utilized very well. She's smart. She knows a lot of stuff. She's acid-tongued and has a great wit. It's very easy to see why the guys hang out with her."

"It doesn't matter whether or not Elaine's a woman," observed Louis-Dreyfus's husband, Brad Hall, who produced the critical favorite *Brooklyn Bridge*. "She has the same lusts and feelings that all guys have. The only woman-specific thing about her is her genitalia."

Louis-Dreyfus says the birth of their son, Henry, in 1992 changed her life. While she considers herself an aggressive actor, motherhood is now her top priority. "I love my job," she explained, "I find it creatively fulfilling, but it's just show business."

The *Seinfeld* team has accommodated her and Henry; during the last, visible months of her pregnancy, Julia was shot from the shoulders up in "The Keys." In other episodes, she was photographed carrying large objects or wearing loose clothing. With the exception of long shooting days, Louis-Dreyfus brings Henry to a nursery on the set so she can be near him.

Even though she and Brad forgo the fancy Hollywood party lifestyle, there are not enough hours in the day.

"I'm at the end of my rope all the time," she confided to a reporter. "It is very difficult, but it's great too. I love my husband, and I love my son, and I love my job. It's not like I'm juggling a bunch of things I hate, but there are tons of things I have to sacrifice all the time. It's nothing but a daily sacrifice, whether it's exercising or going to the movies or getting reading done."

Despite her many years in improv, sketch comedy, and her award-winning work on *Seinfeld*, Louis-Dreyfus says she is not a comedian. She has never written her own material and doesn't even consider herself particularly funny.

"People think I'm going to be real funny right away," she told an interviewer. "I get asked where I've done stand-up, which, of course, I've never done. It's not like I'm one of these people who's 'on.' I have a sort of humorous bent on things."

On the debut episode of *Later With Greg Kinnear*, Louis-Dreyfus took one look at the awkward set, which separated the host from the guest with a large table, and quipped, "I feel like I'm here for a job interview."

Outside of *Seinfeld*, Julia turned up on *The Single Guy* (of which Brad is the producer) as "danger girl," a thrill-seeking girlfriend of star Jonathan Silverman. A previous episode featured Julia's "guest voice" on Silverman's answering machine.

As for feature films, Julia costarred with Billy Crystal and Robin Williams in *Father's Day* (1996) and took on a small but memorable role in Woody Allen's *Deconstructing Harry* (1997).

In public situations, Louis-Dreyfus is constantly recognized by fans who have trouble separating her from her sitcom persona. Even with Brad and Henry in tow, fans call her "Elaine" and wonder if Jerry, George, and Kramer cannot be far away. Although they share some traits—successful, intelligent, sexy—Louis-Dreyfus leaves the character behind on the set when the day's work is over.

Louis-Dreyfus prefers her two-story white-stucco Spanish-style house near Los Angeles to the Manhattan apartment lifestyle of her character. The spacious home, which was built by an artist couple in the late 1920s, allows Louis-Dreyfus to indulge her passion for cooking fish, pasta, "and a beautiful goat cheese salad."

Other interests include antique shopping and collecting, although toting a toddler has limited her outings lately.

Louis-Dreyfus also makes time for causes in which she believes. She's likely to show up at a National Earth Day Rally or alongside Candice Bergen and Vice President Al Gore as a presenter at the Environmental Media Awards show. In 1994, she and costar Alexander gave two live readings of *Bunny Bunny*, to benefit the charity that Gilda Radner set up to aid cancer patients and their families.

The closest that clean-living Louis-Dreyfus has come to scandal was an incident in March 1993, when she was instructed to park her car one day in Tom Arnold's spot in Studio City (where *Seinfeld* and *Roseanne* are shot). In the days that followed, Roseanne and her then-husband allegedly left a series of obscene notes and Polaroids on her car and even soaped obscenities on her windshield, even after she parked her car elsewhere. Tensions—and voices—were raised when Louis-Dreyfus and Jason Alexander confronted the Arnolds, but the storm eventually died down.

Yet it is Louis-Dreyfus's free spirit and appeal to women that people remember most (Clairol appropriately made her their "Nice 'N Easy Girl" for commercials). As Elaine, she has created a character women want to be and men want to date.

Julia Louis-Dreyfus: In Her Own Words

On motherhood: "I'm not conventionally religious, but there's nothing like having a child to make you more spiritual."

On Jerry Seinfeld: "What's remarkable about Jerry is that he takes his work very seriously, yet at the same time he realizes what it is. We are not solving the economy and we are not curing cancer. We are just trying to make a good joke."

On Jason Alexander: "Jason is not angst-ridden like George. And he's a great dancer. I don't think George even knows how to dance."

On male comics vs. female comics: "I think men who are funny are encouraged to be funny. And I think women who are funny—it's not that they're discouraged from it, but it's not considered in a social sense feminine."

On Woody Allen (her director and costar in *Hannah and Her Sisters*): "I was so intimidated to be in his presence. It was unbelievable."

On playing Elaine: "It's probably the best job I'll ever have. It's maybe the best job there is."

On television: "I don't have the time to watch television, and I don't really like television, so I don't really watch."

On her appearance: "Sometimes I think I'm sexy. Then sometimes I think I'm an old bag."

On the pressures of success: "Actually, I feel pressure not to be seduced by the show's success. See, once you get to a certain point and people will laugh at everything you do, it's easy to fall into the trap where you try to get away with less work."

Meet Michael Richards

One thing about Michael Richards, *Seinfeld*'s Kramer: he knows how to make an impression.

More than a decade after his work on *Fridays*, the early-eighties ABC late-night variety show, Richards is still remembered by TV buffs as the overgrown kid in the backyard whose adventures with toy soldiers usually ended up in flames.

Viewers may also remember when Jay Leno—then guest host of *The Tonight Show*—featured Richards as "Dick Williams, Fitness Trainer to the Stars," in a 1989 skit. The sketch, which featured a wacked-out trainer fumbling through a routine, was so funny that even Leno looked like he was ready to crack up. "I had no rehearsal, nothing," Richards recalled. "I improvised most of that . . . dragging equipment down there: barbells, a rowing machine; cigarette in hand and this outfit which was a woman's Olympic swimsuit that I wore with some shorts, black socks, and street shoes."

It was Jerry Seinfeld who recommended Richards to Leno in the first place. And when he and Larry David saw the bit on TV, they brought Richards in to read for Kramer. And he auditioned standing on his head!

"During the audition, while I was reading, I had a sense of the lines.

So I started doing headstands while I was talking," he remembered in an interview with NBC's *Dateline*. "And during one of the headstands I fell over, onto a table, crashed to the floor, and just went on with my dialogue as if nothing had happened. And they [Jerry and Larry] were just roaring. And that was Kramer."

"I found a bit of the character during that reading," he said. "I got a bigger laugh doing that than what I got with the dialogue."

"They wanted an off-the-wall specialist," he recalled. "That's what I do. That's why I got the part."

"This is not the way I *amuse* myself," he told Leno several years later on *The Tonight Show*. "This is the way I *am*."

Richards grew up in the Los Angeles suburb of Van Nuys. His father, an electrical engineer, died when he was a toddler, leaving his mother, a medical librarian, to raise Michael by herself.

Before *Seinfeld*, TV audiences saw Michael Richards get physical on ABC's *Fridays*. (© 1995 Capital Cities/ABC)

As a kid, Richards perfected his comic entrances by mimicking a friend who had crashed his bike into a tree. "Every time I saw him, I would ride my bike into a tree," Richards recalled. "That was my greeting. It cracked everyone up . . . the fool is always the one who

143

takes the fall for everyone else. Everybody laughs at their own fall as it's performed by the clown."

Richards, a self-described "clown who has sought attention since eighth grade," enjoyed drama class at Thousand Oaks High School, and played the Scarecrow in a production of *The Wizard of Oz*. Richards boasts that his high school yearbook said of him "Funniest man alive."

Richards earned a degree in theater from the California Institute of the Arts. Upon graduating, he appeared in several productions with the San Diego Repertory Company. Later he starred in *American Clock* and *Wild Oats* at the Mark Taper Forum in Los Angeles. But the call of comedy was getting louder—especially when hanging out with one of his closest friends.

"Ed Begley Jr. and I, when we were together, were always making everyone laugh," Richards recalled. "People would say, 'You guys ought to get up on stage somewhere.' " They teamed up and worked out a routine at the famed Troubadour.

With a lifelong interest in comedy (his influences include Jonathan Winters, Red Skelton, and Don Rickles), Richards continued to perform stand-up routines in 1979, and appeared nightly for nine months at clubs like The Comedy Store and the Improv. Billy Crystal gave him his first "paying job" on HBO's *The Billy Crystal Special*. He spent the next two and a half years on *Fridays*.

Richards's TV credits included a regular role on the syndicated show *Marblehead Manor*, guest appearances on *The Larry Sanders Show, Bob Hope: The First 90 Years, St. Elsewhere, Miami Vice, Hill Street Blues, Cheers, Night Court, It's a Living, Sidekicks, Scarecrow and Mrs. King*, and the miniseries *Fresno*. Richards also kept busy with five pilot shows, which unfortunately (or fortunately, depending on your perspective) were never picked up by the networks.

Kramer was an early favorite on *Seinfeld* and is still the show's trademark character. He is the only *Seinfeld* character to warrant his own poster— "The Kramer"—a copy of the portrait from 1992's "The Letter." (In that episode, the pretentious art lover who bought the painting commented, "His struggle is man's struggle . . . He's a loathsome, offensive brute, yet I can't look away.") Kramer was also nominated as TV's All-Time Favorite Nosy Neighbor on a CBS special, *TV's All-Time Favorites.*

A recent stop on the information superhighway found Michael Richards's picture the most popular male photo to download among America Online subscribers, with a hot streak of 275 downloads in three weeks (Sharon Stone was the most popular female photo with some 1,300 downloads).

However, Richards's views on fame have shifted somewhat since *Seinfeld* took off. In 1993 he told an interviewer that being recognized by fans was just part of the job: "They just say, 'Look, there's Kramer.' They don't go, 'Look, there's Michael Richards'—forget it. As far as I'm concerned, I am Kramer. And I should be Kramer. I must be Kramer. I have this responsibility to maintain that character because these people, they want Kramer."

But just a few weeks later, riding the crest of a wave of critical and popular success on *Seinfeld*, Richards distinguished himself from the zany character: "Ben Kingsley is *not* Gandhi."

In 1993, his stand-up appearance at the Montreal International Comedy Festival sold out 2,200 seats in less than two hours. "People expected to see Kramer," he told *Entertainment Weekly*. "But my act, sort of a nontraditional stand-up act where I tell stories, wasn't about Kramer. And I got a standing ovation. That was gratifying."

Still, the success of *Seinfeld* has given Richards peace of mind. "I don't have to work just for the money," he explained. "It's a tremendous change. I'm pretty humble. I won't go out and buy a big home or anything. I like to save money, invest a bit, pay things off. I don't have any bills. So I can get back to my life with the theater, improve as an actor."

Richards, the divorced dad of a college-aged daughter, Sophia, says the secret to raising a child is just like acting—being open.

"I've seen other parents restrict their children in the name of perfection," he said. "It's criminal. My daughter wanted to go to her prom wearing black leather and motorcycle boots. And she wanted thirteen earrings in her ear. Now, what are you going to do? Say no? That's how she wants to be. She was the hit of the whole scene, because she was herself."

Unlike Kramer's deliberate, over-the-top speech pattern, Richards's is more careful, more pensive. One interviewer described his speech as "virtually somnambulistic."

"I suspect that in the next ten years I'll be doing things far different from Kramer," he told an interviewer. "Though I *am* looking for comedies. I'm fascinated by comedy, but I'm an actor, so I'm just as moved by a scene in Tennessee Williams. But it would be hard for an audience for me to go from Kramer to running around with a gun or showing some shadowy side of me. Eventually, that will happen."

Richards, whose favorite shows are *Columbo* and *Murder, She Wrote*, would like to develop a show of his own. "I'd play a private investigator with a sidekick," he explained. "Like *Dragnet*, in a sense. The stories are real capers.

Meet Michael Richards

Michael protects the plate against the advances of Sharon Stone in *Baseball Relief*, an early nineties variety special for charity. (Doug Hyun/Fox)

About a guy who went to a private detective school in California and admires Sherlock Holmes, watches all his movies."

Richards is also forging out a movie career. His credits include *Coneheads*; *So I Married an Ax Murderer*; *Airheads*; *Problem Child*; *UHF*; *Whoops, Apocalypse*; *Transylvania 6-5000*; and *Young Doctors in Love*. "I'm interested in doing features," Richards said. "I love the moviemaking business. I like the medium, I like the way you can get at what you do. [By contrast,] television is so fast."

Movies also give Richards more time to work on his character and his delivery. And although his movies have tended to be critical or box-office disappointments, the consensus was that the material was way below Richards's level. "Michael Richards has a unique talent, which needed to find a place," explained Jerry Seinfeld. "Before this show, nobody was using him properly. He's like this engine, just running and running. It's not in gear, it's not driving anything. And if you don't hook it up with something, it's going to turn on you. Having a talent is a kill-or-be-killed thing. Especially comedic talent. It has to be focused on other people, or it turns on you in the most vicious way."

Although his characters are funny, Richards is nothing short of intense when it comes to shooting a scene—a fact that surprises some casual onlookers. And while he

Michael makes (what else?) a big entrance at the MTV Music Awards. (Vinnie Zuffante/Star File)

The Ultimate Collectible

Michael Richards says the *Seinfeld* marketing machine missed the boat by not publishing Kramer's coffee-table book about coffee tables. The book—which Kramer dreams up and pitches to Elaine's boss in "The Cigar Store Indian," and then promotes on *Live With Regis and Kathie Lee* in "The Opposite"—would have made a great collectible, he said.

"I always thought it was a good idea," he explained to the *Los Angeles Times*. "The book had a nice cover of me; I had a pipe." It also had foldout legs that made the book itself into a coffee table.

Unfortunately, he left it behind when he and Jerry Seinfeld went on location in New York to the set of *Live With Regis and Kathie Lee.*

"I accidentally left it at the studio," Richards recalled. "I don't know who got it. As I got into the car, I said, 'Jeez, who got that book?' And no one knew. Somebody clipped it. Forty, fifty years from now, that'll be real collectible."

studies the comic timing of idols Buster Keaton and Peter Sellers, his perfectionist attitude keeps him from watching any of his work on TV or in the movies—including *Seinfeld*.

"I'm so critical of what I do because I always inevitably see more that could have been done. And it can drive me insane," he told an interviewer.

His first dramatic movie role—playing a man suffering from delusional paranoia—in Diane Keaton's *Unstrung Heroes* won critical reviews for Richards, exposing a serious side that is overshadowed by the Kramer character.

Like Seinfeld, Richards brings his own experiences into the show. Just as Jerry injects personal mementos into the set (pictures of his nephew adorn the fridge), Richards suggested hanging a mountain bike in the background. A real-life biking enthusiast, environmentally conscious Richards uses a two-thousand-dollar custom-built bike to commute to and from the set. It was he who suggested to the show's production designer, Thomas Azzari, that a bike would be more interesting than just another bookcase in Jerry's apartment. Richards now rides "purely for pleasure," after a bad fall during practice for a downhill race, aptly named the Kamikaze, changed his tune a couple of years ago.

"I went off the side of the mountain and fell through an oak tree, which broke my fall," he recalled. "I got up and heard a voice in my head say, 'You just can't ride like this.'" Fortunately, there are fewer risks involved in another passion: yoga, which helps him relax before and after showtime.

Just as important as his formal training and influences, Richards incorporates the character elements from everyday people he observes. "I love to go down to the Santa Monica Pier and people-watch," he explained. "I'm fascinated by unusual walks or ways of dress."

Like his castmates, Richards also finds time to support worthy causes, including Comic Relief. He starred in Fox's *Baseball Relief: An All-Star Comedy Salute* with Jerry Seinfeld, Sharon Stone, and other celebs in Comic Relief's National Pediatric Care Program for Homeless Children.

"In many ways, I'm a lightener," Richards explained. "I'm here to lighten the load. That's my task. And it lightens my load too, because I'm able to laugh at myself."

Michael Richards: In His Own Words

On home life: "I love cranking up the heater on the pool, getting it up to 90 degrees, and swimming around naked. A return to the womb. Then, when I got the bill, I said, 'My God. Forget it.' Now, it's better to soak in the tub. It's a lot cheaper."

On his best feature: "I would say that it's that I'm really beginning to enjoy life now . . . I'm reaping the harvest of putting years into this business. Coming into my own, where opportunities are arising. Helping me get more at what I can do. So my best feature comes out of that, a vitality to create."

On his job: "I'm an eccentricity specialist."

On his hair: "It's electric. It just goes whoooom! It's interesting. It just took its own shape. It's fascinating. It *is* like a back-to-nature look, isn't it?"

On Kramer: "Sometimes I feel like I'm riding the tail of a comet. I have a picture of Kramer in my den because I look at him as a real friend. I'm going to miss him when he's not around."

Hello . . . Newman:
A Conversation
With Wayne Knight

It only takes a few minutes for Newman to set the *Seinfeld* world upside down. And that's what makes him the most fascinating character on the show.

From his rude "Hello . . . Jerry" greeting to his cold, matter-of-fact observations (in "The Pick," he instantaneously spots Elaine's nipple in the infamous Christmas-card debacle), the sweaty, frenetic postal worker represents the loner time-bomb in all of us. We've seen Newman conspire with Kramer to sell an old man's records ("The Old Man"), steal Jerry's hair ("The Barber"), and stand beside George in his crusade against pull-in parking ("The Parking Space"). And while everyone else in the *Seinfeld* universe was tuned to the pilot episode of *Jerry*, Newman had dozed off in front of a Yankees game ("The Pilot"). Newman's comment to Keith Hernandez, "Nice game, pretty boy," set the stage for the legendary "June 14, 1987, Spitting Incident," and one of the greatest *Seinfeld* episodes of all time, "The Boyfriend."

But the brilliant character of Newman was only partly created on the printed page. To bring him to life, Jerry Seinfeld and Larry David chose Wayne Knight. Following his *Seinfeld* debut in January 1992 in "The Suicide," Knight became an instant sensation as the show's preeminent recurring character, and has gone on to appear in a handful of blockbuster dramatic films, NBC's *The Second Half* and *Against the Grain*, and the short-lived Fox comedy series, *The Edge*.

Despite his busy schedule of movies, TV shows, TV movies, and pilots, Wayne was nice enough to grant *Nothing: The Newsletter for Seinfeld Fans* an exclusive phone interview from Los Angeles. Here are the highlights from that chat . . .

Okay, let me just start off with a few basic questions. How did you get contacted to be on *Seinfeld*?

Actually, what happened was they had done one episode in which Newman appeared without [the audience] seeing his face. The voice was Larry David or somebody off-camera, and Newman was threatening to commit suicide. After that, they decided that they wanted to show him.

The first episode that he actually appeared in was ["The Suicide"] when Jerry's neighbor is in a coma and he is trying to decide at what point it is proper to make a hit on the girlfriend of the guy that is in a coma. So I came in and auditioned. Newman at that time was a totally different character, whose father owned the building. He was kind of in the building as the son of the landlord. We kind of ad-libbed around that event, and they liked it, and I got the job of doing him the first time. Most of that script was thrown out—they simplified it. [Michael Richards] and I were in one scene in the hospital room. They were just looking at Michael and I sitting there together, you know, looking like something from an earlier World's Fair, I being the globe and him being the needle, and there was just some kind of chemistry there. They kept bringing me back.

What is it about you and Kramer together that is really funny?

Well, the thing that is interesting is that Newman really idolizes Kramer and believes that Kramer is a really smart guy and actually kind of needs him for grounding. Newman can go frantic and fly off the deep end and is really kind of depressive. Kramer is like his only real friend. So this gives Kramer the opportunity of playing genius to Newman, and at the same time they argue over everything because they each think they are right.

I remember the episode when you were selling the used records back ["The Old Man"] and the episode when you were both staking out the investor you thought was on drugs—"The Sniffing Accountant." That was some great teamwork there.

Yeah, well you know, I think Newman's function on the show used to be more with Kramer, in Kramer's world, and as of late come in as an irritant to Jerry directly. So, you know, it is a slightly different usage of the character . . . I always find there's a lot of avenue for that kind of grand, physical stuff when dealing with Michael.

When you are in the hall and you are about to enter Jerry's apartment, how do you get ready to be Newman?

Well, you have to stick a thumbtack right firmly up your ass. Ooowwww that hurts! Then you go in there and you're ready to bite somebody's head off. For some reason, I hooked into Newman early. There's a sense of blind aggression out of Newman and it's kind of like you know you can venture to the dark side. And then when I'm done I feel refreshed and like I've cleansed myself of some of my evil side.

I think it's fantastic that he's a postal worker.
When that was revealed that was one of my favorite moments.

I absolutely love the line in "The Lip Reader" about "When you control the mail you control information." That's got to be a classic. Now, was there ever an explanation of why Jerry and Newman have this confrontation when they see each other? I mean, was it ever explained or do they just not like each other?
Well, you know, there is an event, there is something that happened, but it hasn't been explained. I mean, one of the good things about the show is that you don't spell everything out. And there are people that you have these pre-existing feelings about and, you know, you're privy to them as an audience, but you don't have the whole story. It makes it funny. I mean, even Jerry's mother hates Newman. There is just something about the Seinfeld family. They can't stand Newman.

The first time I remember seeing you was in one of my favorite movies, *Dead Again.* I thought that was great, and ever since then you've been in some big movies. Tell me a little bit about the movie experience.
Well, actually what I like is that the movies tend to be serious films. I may have a lighter or somewhat comedic role within them, but they are not comedy movies, and most of the television work is comedy.

It gives me some kind of variety of a career that makes me feel like I'm an actor, you know, and not just a type doing what I do on television. I got lucky enough, I had done some small roles in films, but nothing of any consequence. One of my very good friends is Emma Thompson, and when she and Ken Branagh were deciding that they were going to do an American film, Ken came across Scott Frank's script of *Dead Again* and decided to do it. He literally called and said, "You know there's a part for you. Do you want to do it?" And I said, "Well, yes!"

So that opened the door for feature films for me because once a director has said, "Yes, you're qualified to do these features," you get in for other auditions. While I was doing *Dead Again* out here in Los Angeles I had gotten in to see Oliver Stone for *JFK* and gotten in to see Paul Verhoven for *Basic Instinct* while I was doing a film at the same time over at Paramount. So I think there is a momentum that happens when work begets work. So I really give Ken great credit for starting my film career rolling.

They turned *Star Trek: The Next Generation* into a movie franchise. Any chance of turning Seinfeld into a movie franchise?

Actually, you know, I think that they should combine the two. I think there would be a nice *Planet of the Seinfelds*. If you notice in our long episodes it is very hard to tie all the threads together, especially in the way that Jerry and Larry David work, so that every little side trip kind of leads back to Rome at the end of the episode. For you to try to do that for ninety minutes or two hours, I don't think you could do it. Whether or not Jerry would be interested in doing films not based on these characters, I don't know, but I would tend to doubt that this will ever be a feature.

Newman's Greatest Hits

"The Raincoats"
At a showing of *Schindler's List*, Newman spots Jerry moving on his girlfriend Rachel "like the storm troopers into Poland," and tells both Jerry's and Rachel's parents.

"The Boyfriend"
Newman recalls igniting the June 14, 1987, spitting incident by cursing at Mets relief pitcher Roger McDowell and pouring a beer on his head.

"The Barber"
Newman agrees to steal a strand of Jerry's hair for his barber in exchange for a year's worth of free haircuts . . . and a comb.

"The Old Man"
Newman and Kramer conspire to sell a collection of vintage records owned by Sid Fields, an elderly man with whom George volunteered to spend time.

"The Big Salad"
Jerry can't handle the fact that his girlfriend, Margaret, used to date Newman—and that *he* dumped *her*.

"The Switch"
Newman is caught making out with Kramer's mother, Babs.

"The Doodle"
After he finds his apartment infested with fleas, Jerry discovers a telltale Chunky candy wrapper under the couch and traces the problem to Newman.

"The Scofflaw"
Newman turns himself in after years of illegally parking his 1979 brown Dodge Diplomat.

"The Reverse Peephole"
Newman is nearly evicted when the super suspects him of sleeping with his wife (although Newman brags "There is very little sleeping going on!").

"The Betrayal"
Newman reveals the secret of ZIP Codes to his beautiful blonde girlfriend: "They're meaningless!"

"The Butter Shave"
Newman salivates at the thought of a buttery hot Kramer boiling in his hot tub; and has delusions of Kramer's head on an oven-roasted turkey.

In the papers here in New York, they were previewing the one-hour *Schindler's List* episode, and the last sentence was, "... and plenty of Newman." How do you feel about being the Fifth Beatle of the *Seinfeld* show?

Well, I don't mind the Pete Best role as long as I don't have the Stu Sutcliffe role. As long as I can live through the experience, then I think it is fine with me. Early on, I really wanted to kind of latch on to the show like Kelsey Grammer had on *Cheers*—kind of like step in in the third season and then just hook on and stay with it. But I came to realize that Newman is kind of like seasoning in the stew. He's not the meat and he's not going to be. And instead of being resentful or sad that I don't have a bigger part in it, I feel lucky to have had any part in it. So I am more than pleased to have that kind of designation because I think I've gotten more notoriety on the work of Newman than just about anything else I've done, and I might just show up for a good thirty seconds of an episode.

And that might make the episode.

Well it's very nice. It's kind of pivotal. It's not long in duration, but it can be pivotal.

Like in that one-hour *Schindler's List* episode ["The Raincoats"], it was you who pretty much screwed up the whole hour and you were only in it for a few minutes.

Yes, well I've made a whole career out of screwing things up. You know basically I screw up Jurassic Park, I screw up Jerry's life, I screw up. I'm the screw-up guy.

I had read that you were the first one to be cast in *Jurassic Park*.

Umm, myself and the kids. Yeah. I was about to sign a deal with *The*

Second Half to do the series, which would have made it impossible for me to do the movie. So they locked me up so that I was able to do the film, and then we worked both schedules around each other. Apparently [Spielberg] had seen me in *Basic Instinct* and saw me covered in sweat, and thought, "Imagine that as being rain, and imagine that being a dinosaur instead of a woman with her legs spread. Yes, this could work!"

The Real TV People

$\mathbf{B}$y now we all know that Jerry Seinfeld, the stand-up comedian who cowrote an NBC pilot, is the inspiration for the character "Jerry Seinfeld," a stand-up comedian who wrote an NBC pilot (about a stand-up comedian named Jerry Seinfeld . . .). But who inspired the other characters?

George Costanza

Larry David, cocreator, executive producer, and head writer of *Seinfeld*, admits that the morose George Costanza character is based on him—everything from the low self-esteem and doomsday philosophy right down to the bald pate and glasses. Larry's brand of angst is vented through George's self-effacing observational humor.

For example, when David won the Emmy in 1993 for Best Writing in a Comedy Series, he clenched the statue, took a deep breath, and declared, "This is all well and good, but I'm still bald."

A former stand-up comic, David's club routine included a bit about people with body temperatures so high they could melt butter on their foreheads. But he was probably more popular with other comedians than with comedy-club patrons, whom he would often berate for no apparent reason.

David worked as a writer-performer with Michael Richards on ABC's *Fridays* from 1980–82 and then joined *SNL* for the 1984–85 season as a staff writer, although legend has it that none of his *SNL* skits made it to air.

"Our senses of humor dovetail in such a way that the words sound right coming out of my mouth," said Seinfeld, "but most of the time they're his words. I'd say 90 percent of the show comes from Larry."

Among David's writings is an unproduced screenplay, *Prognosis Negative*, a dark comedy that shares a title with the movie Jerry sees with George (and then again with Elaine) in "The Dog."

"The person I was then is the person I am now, only with more money," David told an interviewer. "I work so hard now, so unrelentingly, that I don't have much time to think about myself the way I used to, barely have time to know how miserable I really am. That's the one good thing about working on TV."

Elaine Benes

Seinfeld and David had no intention of creating a female lead when they wrote what would become the *Seinfeld* pilot. But after pressure from NBC brass to add a good-looking love interest, the duo compromised by adding an ex-girlfriend who still hangs out with Jerry.

Although she is a composite of several women friends of the show's creative duo, Elaine is loosely based on Jerry's real-life ex-girlfriend, comedian Carol Leifer, who neither confirms nor denies the connection.

The real deal: Larry David, Carol Leifer, and Jerry Seinfeld inspired three out of four of *Seinfeld*'s characters. (*Los Angeles Times*/Robert Durell)

"I kind of live Elaine's lifestyle, in being single and being from New York," Leifer confessed to *Newsday*, "and having these kind of Elaine experiences. But I always tell people it's really Kramer who's modeled after me."

Like Elaine, Leifer is still a close-but-platonic ally of Seinfeld. "We went out so long ago," she explained, "that it's kind of like another lifetime, and we've been friends so much longer. But I think it's a great way to have a friendship, because if you've already been out and taken care of that, any curiosity or whatever, you've gotten out of your system."

A stand-up comic, Leifer made the same circuits as comedians like Seinfeld and Paul Reiser, a fellow student at SUNY Binghamton, whom she also dated. In the late 1980s, she hosted a comedy show on VH-1. But Leifer found the club dates lonely and tiresome. After one-too-many nights in a "Chuckle Hut" (her name for the generic comedy clubs of the 1980s), she quit the road and accepted a writing job offer from Seinfeld and David, who liked the fact that Leifer had no sitcom credentials.

"I think definitely we have a similar sensibility," she once related to the *Today* show's Al Roker. "Well, anything to get out of clubs. Like, do you want to work at the Comedy Pouch or work on a network primetime hit show? It's a very tough choice."

Leifer has done occasional stand-up performances since joining *Seinfeld*, opening for Jerry on his 1994 minitour and doing some corporate dates for Intel. Leifer, the show's story editor, even showed up as an annoying receptionist in "The Kiss Hello," where she hassled Elaine and George.

Kramer

Seinfeld fans are more than surprised they're often shocked—to find out that there is a real-life Kramer dwelling in the apartments of Manhattan. His first name's not Cosmo (it's Kenny), and he claims to be more animated and eccentric than the Kramer played by Michael Richards.

Kramer—yes, he answers to Kramer—has lived in the same apartment since the seventies, the same place, in fact, where he met and lived next door to Larry David.

Kenny "The Real" Kramer is now leading tours of the places that inspired the *Seinfeld* show. That's friend and former neighbor Larry David over Kenny's left shoulder on the Kramer "Wall of Fame." (Van Nostrand Archive)

Unlike his TV counterpart, Kenny's hair does not defy gravity. But like the character portrayed by Michael Richards, Kenny is funny and talkative, with entrepreneurism and showbusiness in his blood.

One gets the sense that fifty-something Kenny is just settling down after a wild ride through life. In the seventies and early eighties he worked as a "rock and roll" comic, performing raunchy sex-and-drugs monologues as opening act to the likes of ZZ Top, Average White Band, Three Dog Night, Kiss, and others. In the eighties, Kramer left the comedy stage "before the boom" when his disco novelty jewelry "caught on." In 1996, he caused a media sensation by creating Kramer's Reality Tour, a multimedia guided bus tour tracing the steps of Seinfeld and David in the days leading up to *Seinfeld*.

A consummate *Seinfeld* fan, Kenny knows and stays in touch with the *Seinfeld* camp and never misses an episode. One Thursday evening he invited a curious, note-taking *Seinfeld* fan to his place for an interview. And since it got late, his guest got to watch *Seinfeld* with the "real-life" Kramer.

Do you call yourself Kramer? What do people call you?

Most of my friends call me Kenny. Some of them call me Kramer. Larry has always called me Kramer—or Krame—or Double K or K2 or Doctor K. I find that when people talk about me they say, "Hey, did you hear what Kramer did?" That's how the name came to be in the show. That's why the character isn't named Kenny.

When did you find out that your friend and neighbor, Larry David, was creating a sitcom?

I found out the night that Jerry came to him and said to him, "You got any ideas for a TV show?"

Jerry, as a comedian, had idolized Larry. So they went to a diner, around the corner from where the Improv used to be, and they sat down and had a cup of coffee. And Larry came up with this concept: "You're a comedian, and you work forty minutes a night. What happens in your life the other twenty-three hours and twenty minutes? That could be the show." It was just about the way it looked on television.

And then Larry said [to me], "I want to have a neighbor, and I'm going to base him on you. Is that okay?" I said, "Sure, be my guest."

Did you ask to play Kramer?

Sure! Are you kidding? I said, "Larry, listen. You're writing a character based on me that looks like me, that talks like me, that has ideas that are my philosophies—how about me playing Kramer?" And he says, "No you can't play Kramer . . . You're not right for it." I said, "What do you mean I'm not right for it? I am Kramer!"

Chicago Singles Do "The Kramer"

The Twist, The Electric Slide, The Kramer.

The Kramer? The evolution of modern dance came head-to-head with *Seinfeld* culture in 1994 when the *Chicago Sun-Times* gave a new twist to singles dances—including a new hip-hop song and dance inspired by none other than Cosmo Kramer. The paper's annual "Zazz Bash," named for author and advice columnist Jeffrey Zaslow, turned the Grand Ballroom at Navy Pier into one of the city's largest singles parties ever.

A crowd of 6,400 Chicago-area singles turned out for the meet and greet, to celebrate the dating ritual in the age of *Seinfeld*. Danny Bonaduce (TV's Danny Partridge) and local TV personalities Roberta Gonzales and Nesita Kwan emceed the festivities, including lookalike contests, soundalike contests, a cereal-eating competition, and a gyroscope flight-simulator designed to give partygoers a Krameresque coif.

Zaslow said *Seinfeld* was a natural choice for a singles-party theme. In a survey of the previous year's partygoers, 70 percent said they would make a fitting character on *Seinfeld*, he explained.

Emcee Danny Bonaduce measures the "grace" of an Elaine lookalike at Chicago's Zazz Bash '94. (*Chicago Sun-Times*)

"*Seinfeld* is the ultimate singles show," he said. "This is the ultimate singles party."

Steve Rashid and Kevin Connelley of Chicago's Hothouse Music came up with the tune, while Cheri Coons, another Chicagoan, penned the lyrics.

He got a Cuban cigar
He got a babe in the car
He got hit by a loogie
By a baseball star

The catchy chorus asks:

Outrageous
Bodacious
Ooo, Kramer
What makes your hair stand up?

Giddyap! Kramer doubles get down to the sounds of "The Kramer." (*Chicago Sun-Times*)

The dance, which features erratic movements and flailing limbs, was choreographed by Bea Rashid, who led revelers in the dance's official debut.

Michael Richards even sent audiotaped dance tips to the crowd: "Keep a lot of beverages in your body and don't eat cereal before you dance."

Proceeds of the event went to the Sun-Times Charity Trust, the Chicago Fund on Aging and Disability, and the Chicago-area chapter of the Alzheimer's Association.

The host said Zazz Bashes have led to at least fourteen marriages. But *Seinfeld* fans know they've probably led to many more Good Meeting Stories and Dating Decathlons.

So that was just like on the episode "The Pilot."

Exactly like "The Pilot." But I gotta go with Larry. Michael Richards turned out pretty phenomenal. He really brought the whole physical thing to the character. The words were all there, but without those entrances, without the things that Michael is able to do with his body, the character would not have taken on the life that it took on.

So you actually lived across the hall from Larry David . . .

Right.

Did you barge in?

We kept our doors open at all times. We were continuously walking back and forth.

Did you borrow a lot of stuff—or food—from him?

Actually it was kind of the other way around. I lived here with my daughter, and I always kept my refrigerator full of food. Larry's refrigerator looked like a hooker's refrigerator, with a half-bottle of ginger ale and an old lemon. Larry used to have a list on my refrigerator door. And every time he took something, he'd mark down what it was, because he never wanted me to feel he was taking advantage of my food. "Mallomars . . . There are ten of these in a box, at two dollars a box, so that's twenty cents apiece. Two Mallomars, forty cents."

What things on *Seinfeld* do you recognize or give you a feeling a déjà vu?

They are too numerous to mention. Larry has an eye that when he sees something, he remembers it and it turns up. There's just loads and loads and loads of stuff that actually happened.

A typical example was "The Tape" [in which George asks a Chinese delivery boy to call China and order him a new baldness remedy, and Kramer then checks his progress with a videocamera]. That was exactly the way it happened. I said, "Call up the Chinese restaurant. That guy, he hardly speaks English. He must speak Chinese. We'll get him to call China and we'll get the information." Bob Shaw [a comedy writer who has written for and appeared on *Seinfeld*] was the other guy involved in this. He actually saw it on CNN. So they called CNN and they got the number. They got the delivery boy to call. They had to go to the Bank of China to get a money order. When the stuff arrived it smelled like shit—a sulfur kind of rotten-egg odor. So I said, "Before you start putting the stuff on, let's do some 'before' pictures." Every time he thought there was some growth, I said, "Let's go to the videotape." It never worked.

I was in the Jacuzzi the day after that episode aired and these people said, "Did you see *Seinfeld* last night? That was hilarious! How to they think of that stuff? Those writers are just geniuses!" I was laughing to myself because that was exactly the way it happened.

Is Larry really George?

Oh, 100 percent. Larry has a misanthropic sort of personality. He never deserves to be happy. He'll never be happy. Like, if NBC is going to buy the show, that must mean he has a terminal disease of some sort because God is not going to let it happen. And that's the way it's been for Larry. Larry has made a slight change in his life, you know, in that he's so successful now. But as he's made this change to success, so has George, if you noticed. George went from the ranks of the unemployed . . .

To the opposite . . .

He's successful, he's dating models, he's working for the Yankees . . .

The way Jason Alexander plays the character, it seems George—and thus, Larry—can take a joke about his baldness, or his glasses.

Larry has always been very big in self-deprecating humor. The opening joke in Larry's act used to be, "I'll tell you something about good-looking people—we're not well liked."

I see you have a golf bag here. TV Kramer plays. Do you?

Yea.

How about cigars? You like cigars?

Occasionally. That's not really me. That's more Larry's idea.

Mangoes? Peaches?

Yea, I'm very big on fresh fruit. Fresh fruit and salads. I'm sort of a health-freak kind of guy. That part is true. There are maybe fifty or sixty things that have appeared in the show that are all pretty much the way it happened. Also they're very big on names. They'll have a name of a character in the show that is actually the name of a person. I know the president of NBC . . .

Russell Dalrymple?

Right—he was Larry's wife's assistant at Fox. Between Jerry and Larry, they've used up all their friends, all their relatives, their cousins, ex-girlfriends, all of their college friends . . . The Drake.

The Drake?

The Drake is a guy.

The Real TV People

Do they hate the Drake?

They love The Drake. Drake is good. In fact The Drake is the guy who got me my Callaway Big Berthas [a brand of golf clubs]. He's something in advertising.

If you could write a script, what would it be like?

I have an idea for a screenplay about a guy who lives across the hall from this writer . . . Larry David.

If you had a wish for Kramer on the show to do something . . .

He's done just about everything I can imagine.

Crazy Joe Davola

They say "be careful what you ask for—you may get it." That would seem to apply to Joe Davola, a TV production executive formerly with Fox (now at MTV), who begged his pals Larry David and Jerry Seinfeld to use his name on the show.

Over the years, Peter Crombie's characterization of "Crazy Joe Davola," a psychotic failed writer who depends on medication to stay in control, becomes obsessed with Elaine ("The Opera"), kicks Kramer in the head ("The Pitch"), and attacks Jerry *à la* John Wilkes Booth ("The Pilot"). By all accounts, however, the real Joe is not crazy.

Is it weird watching *Seinfeld* on TV, where bits of your life are played out?

No, not at all. I love it—having a personal relationship with the show and the people. It's not weird at all to me. I guess I'm the number-one fan.

Jerry's New York

Although *Seinfeld* retains the New York edge of its creators and star, the show is actually filmed in Los Angeles. But because the City of New York is itself a character, the writers incorporate a great deal of the New York mentality into just about every script. And, with the exception of some nit-picking by "real" New Yorkers, they manage to maintain the illusion every week.

And although real-life Jerry Seinfeld has taken up in the Hollywood Hills, just a stone's throw from Sharon Stone, he still has the Central Park West apartment he bought in 1988. Both he and TV Jerry, as his character is called on the set, will stay put.

"I don't care how successful the fictional Jerry gets," Seinfeld promised. "He's never moving. No one in New York ever gives up their apartment."

With the exception of brief jaunts to California, the Hamptons, and some out-of-town gigs, TV Jerry's world is the greater metropolitan New York area. Despite initial fears from NBC that the show's urban sensibilities—the subway, bouts with dry cleaners, the importance of fruit stands—would turn off viewers, the network went with it, and even created other shows, such as

Friends and *Mad About You*, to appeal to the same core of young, city-based professionals who first latched on to *Seinfeld*.

"New York is like a pie in the face every day," Seinfeld explained to *New York* magazine. "Walking down the streets of New York is like being in a pie fight. And that's good for your sense of humor."

"To me [New York] is like a huge cocktail party, with all these interesting people and unusual things that are just an arm's length away," he explained. "Even if you're not talking with exactly who you want to be talking with, you can see them right across the room. And you're just glad that you're in the room, you know. That's what a good party's about. It's nice to be in the room."

Of course, Jerry's World is not composed solely of buildings. And for Julia Louis-Dreyfus, a former New York resident, there are other facets of New York that find their way into the show.

"I miss the winter. I miss the cold weather," she told a reporter. "I miss buses, and I miss rude, aggressive people. The people in California are just quietly aggressive and subtly rude."

AP's TV writer, Frazier Moore, says the Big Apple is a favorite setting for sitcoms and cop dramas because it "offers fictional characters a handy, anything-goes latitude. Place them in NYC, at least nominally, and you've got behavioral carte blanche."

So now join our sneaker-wearing host, the man who visits fascinating people in his West Side neighborhood and occasionally bumps into a harried mailman. Mr. Seinfeld—Jerry to his friends and neighbors—has created a new chapter in the book of New York tourist attractions. So hop on a trolley (or even a subway) and wander the world of make-believe known as Jerry's New York.

Manhattan

The Apartment

On TV, Jerry lives at 129 West 81st Street, but the actual building there (a five-story, gray-brick walk-up, where a struggling Jerry Seinfeld lived in a $200-a-month studio) looks nothing like the edifice seen on TV. The real exterior location for Jerry's domain is in Los Angeles, near the corner of Sixth Street and Vermont Avenue. Sharp-eyed fans could tell the building was a product of California by the earthquake reinforcements. By the way, Jerry lives in apartment 5A, Kramer in 5B, and depending on which episode you believe, Newman lives down the hall in either 5E ("The Big Salad") or 5F ("The Doodle"). Early episodes placed Jerry on the third floor of the building, but he's obviously more comfortable two stories higher.

The Improvisation

Although the club has moved to a new location, *Seinfeld* still incorporates the old facade (358 West 44th Street), most likely for sentimental reasons—it was one of Larry's favorite clubs.

Monk's Diner

The coffee shop where the gang gathers to discuss nothing in particular is actually called Tom's Restaurant, and is located at Broadway and 112th Street,

With "Tom's" cropped out of the frame, this Manhattan diner is transformed into Monk's on *Seinfeld*. The exterior was painted yellow after a few seasons. (Van Nostrand Archive)

not far from Columbia University. Only the exterior is used, and it is shot so that the "Tom's" in the name cannot be seen. Longtime fans noticed that the brown exterior was painted yellow a few years into the show. Historical note: Tom's is the namesake of Suzanne Vega's a cappella hit, "Tom's Diner."

Tutti Frutti, Oh Rudy!

How did New York City's current mayor chip away his tough, stony image after winning the 1993 election? PR people? Kissing babies? Nah, he did it by appearing on *Seinfeld*.

While most of the show had been filmed a week earlier, Mayor-elect Rudolph Giuliani shot his cameo part for "The Non-Fat Yogurt" from the site of his victory party, mere hours after his narrow-margin win over incumbent David Dinkins, on the morning of Wednesday, November 3, 1993. The *Seinfeld* team edited in his part, and the show aired the following night. Talk about down to the wire!

In the episode, Giuliani campaigns on a platform that includes cracking down on frozen yogurt shops that fraudulently claim their yogurt is nonfat.

Had the election gone the other way, Dinkins was lined up to do the same cameo role.

No one's really sure why Dinkins lost the election, although it might've had something to do with an idea given to him by an adviser (who got it from Elaine)—that all New Yorkers should wear name tags so they can greet each other on a first-name basis.

Madison Square Garden

A focal point for many New Yorkers, the legendary Garden (Eighth Avenue at 33rd Street) is home to the Knicks, Rangers, and numerous concerts and special events. It is where the gang sees a Rangers-Devils hockey playoff game with Elaine's boyfriend, an enthusiastic New Jersey Devils fan ("The Face Painter"), and the circus ("The Gymnast"), and it's where George and Jerry wanted to go (to see a Knicks game) when they commandeered a limousine home from the airport ("The Limo").

176

NBC Studios

Jerry and George are all too familiar with the NBC offices at 30 Rockefeller Plaza. It's where the duo pitched their idea for "the show about nothing," met NBC president Russell Dalrymple and George's eventual fiancée, Susan, and held auditions for the pilot of *Jerry* ("The Pilot").

NBC Studios is also where Jerry embarrassed himself on the *Today* show by wearing outrageous, billowy pirate garb in "The Puffy Shirt."

Note: NBC is also the home of *Saturday Night Live*, the show that both Jerry Seinfeld and Jason Alexander hosted, and of which Julia Louis-Dreyfus was a cast member. Fans can now buy *Seinfeld* and *SNL* memorabilia in the NBC Store located here.

WNET–Channel 13

WNET (356 West 58th Street) is the New York City public television station that Jerry, Kramer, and George attempted to help out in "The Pledge Drive." However, the evening did not go as well as expected, as George failed to bring Yankee slugger Danny Tartabull, and Uncle Leo demanded the show be stopped when Kramer solicited a $1,500 pledge from Jerry's nana.

Mr. Pitt's Building

This ivy-covered structure, where Elaine worked for Mr. Pitt, is located at the northeast corner of 91st Street and West End Avenue. The doorman, however, is much nicer than the Larry Miller character who vexed Jerry in "The Doorman."

Elaine's Apartment

After she got kicked out of the apartment she subletted in "The Opposite," Elaine presumably moved to 16 West 75th Street, Apartment 2G, where she gave her address to Hop Sing's Chinese restaurant in "The Race."

Pendant Publishing

The publisher that employed Elaine (and briefly, George) and published Kramer's coffee-table book about coffee tables is located at 600 Madison Avenue. However, Elaine's love of Jujyfruits indirectly caused the demise of this company ("The Opposite"). Morty Seinfeld says Harry Fleming used to have an office in the building and there used to be a deli on the first floor ("The Raincoats").

Roosevelt Hospital

This West Side hospital, at 428 West 59th Street, is apparently the gang's favorite. It's where . . .

• Jerry and Kramer watch an operation and accidentally drop a candy into the patient's open body cavity ("The Junior Mint").
• George finds a perfect parking spot only to have a suicide jumper land on his car ("The Bris").
• Kramer thinks he sees a genetically altered "pigman" only to find out he is a pink, hairless car thief who makes off with George's damaged car ("The Bris").

- Jerry tries to cheer up his sick friend Fulton ("The Stand-In").
- Elaine goes for stitches after being bitten by a dog ("The Glasses").
- Kramer promises a sick child that Yankee Paul O'Neill will hit two home runs for him in exchange for a birthday card signed by the Yankee organization ("The Wink").
- George tries to get Marisa Tomei's phone number from Elaine's ill friend ("The Cadillac").
- George begs Susan's cousin—who is in labor—not to name the child Seven ("The Seven").

Plaza Hotel

The Plaza, Fifth Avenue at 59th Street, is the kind of place Sinatra stays in, according to Morty Seinfeld, with free macadamia nuts and even a phone in the john. Elaine was planning to stay there at the expense of a prospective employer (who believed Elaine had come from Florida. But when Jerry's apartment is sprayed for fleas, his visiting parents are invited to take the suite instead. Jerry's parents, with the help of Uncle Leo and Nana, run up a huge tab and ruin Elaine's chance at getting the job ("The Doodle").

Marriott Marquis

This luxury hotel in the heart of Broadway (at 45th Street) is the scene of a benefit for able mentally challenged adults. Kramer scuffles with The Jimmy there and duets with the Velvet Fog himself, Mel Tormé ("The Jimmy").

West Side YMCA

George and Jerry spot Keith Hernandez in the locker room at the West Side Y (5 West 63rd Street) after playing a game of basketball with Kramer. It's also the place where Jerry, George, and Kramer see each other naked for the first time ("The Boyfriend").

Fitzpatrick's Bar and Grill

Fitzpatrick's is the East Side watering hole (1641 Second Avenue) where Keith Hernandez and Elaine flirt and discuss the legendary Game Six ("The Boyfriend") and where George entertains some hard-drinking "bastards" from the Houston Astros front office ("The Hot Tub").

The Metropolitan Opera

Elaine becomes a "beard" for a friend of a friend who is gay, and she falls in love with him after they see *Swan Lake* at the Metropolitan Opera House (aka "The Met") at Lincoln Center, 140 West 65th Street at Columbus Avenue ("The Beard").

New York Public Library

Jerry and George go to the library, Fifth Avenue at 42nd Street, to return a book that is twenty years overdue and find Mr. Heyman, their former gym teacher, who is now homeless, living on the steps ("The Library").

Barney's New York

Elaine accuses this upscale clothing store of installing deceptive "skinny mirrors" in order to make clothing look better on customers. She threatens to turn in store officials to the "department of whatever" for "false reflecting" ("The Secretary").

If the clientele seems dressed up, maybe it's because, as Kramer says, "When you're shopping on Madison Avenue, you don't want to skimp on the swank." Real-life Jerry is one of the many famous clients of the new location, at 61st Street and Madison Avenue.

Royale Pastry Shop

At 237 West 72nd Street, the Royale Pastry Shop is where Jerry and Elaine buy a babka and Jerry vomits after eating a black-and-white cookie ("The Dinner Party").

ABC Studios

Kramer's pal Mickey gets him a job with ABC/Capital Cities (77 West 66th Street) working as a double for an actor on the soap opera *All My Children* ("The Stand-In"). Kramer also started and ended his book tour with a disastrous appearance on *Live With Regis and Kathie Lee* ("The Opposite").

Historical note: Despite his line "Did I tell you this guy was bonkos?" in "The Opposite," Regis Philbin claims he never uses the word "bonkos."

"I've heard of *bonkers* . . . never *bonkos*," Regis later said.

Hotel Edison

George is taken to this stately hotel, at 228 West 47th Street, by a seductive swindler, who handcuffs him to the bed and makes off with his money—$8—and his Moe Ginsburg suit ("The Subway").

Cineplex Odeon Regency

The movie theater, located at 1987 Broadway, is the one in which Newman spies Jerry and Rachel making out in the balcony during a showing of *Schindler's List* ("The Raincoats").

Central Park

A green oasis in the center of Manhattan, Central Park is the site of the show-league game between The Improv and *Rochelle, Rochelle: The Musical* ("The Understudy"), and is home to many monuments and structures, including the zoo in which Kramer gets into an altercation with a chimpanzee named Barry ("The Face Painter"). While filling in for a hansom carriage driver in "The Rye," Kramer explains the park was designed in 1850 by Joe Pepitone and used by Union armies to practice fighting on grass.

Trump Tower

At 725 Fifth Avenue, Trump Tower is one of the country's most famous addresses. Owned by and named for real estate mogul Donald Trump, this glittery complex of offices, stores, and residences is home to Calvin Klein company, which Kramer visits in "The Pez Dispenser" to pitch an idea for a beach-scented fragrance. Kramer returns there with Jerry in "The Pick" to accuse Klein of stealing his idea, but winds up getting a modeling job. Jerry confronts Tia, a model he dated, to tell her he had been scratching—not picking—his nose.

Broadway

Broadway is New York's Theater District, and mecca for Kramer, who professes, "My Broadway is the Broadway of Merman and Martin and Fontaine." Broadway is where Bette Midler appears in *Rochelle, Rochelle: The Musical*; Elaine's close-talking boyfriend Aaron takes the Seinfelds to see *My Fair Lady* ("The Raincoats"); and where George takes Elaine to see the lavish Broadway musical *Guys and Dolls* after Jerry declined to go to a play that might make him look gay—"not that there's anything wrong with that" ("The Outing").

The Soup Stand

Next to Monk's Diner, the most sought after *Seinfeld* spot in New York is probably Soup Kitchen International, at 259-A West 55th Street (near Eighth Avenue), home of a chef known for strict rules and the best soup in the city. For legal reasons, NBC will not confirm that this tiny store was the inspiration for "The Soup Nazi" episode. But the similarity is too great to be a coincidence (and besides, Julia Louis-Dreyfus confirmed the parallel in an interview with the *New York Post*). Soup Man Al Yeganeh has posted rules to keep the line moving at an optimal rate of seven seconds per customer. Deviation from the rules results in revocation of the free fruit or bread.

Even before the episode first aired on November 2, 1995, customers lined up outside the shop for up to forty minutes for their daily fix of soup. These days, customers can expect to wait up to an hour or more for the scrumptious soups, priced anywhere from six dollars for a small cup to thirteen dollars for a large container. As for the nickname, it is hardly a laughing matter for the camera-shy proprietor. Perhaps Kramer had it right when he said the fictional chef is not really a Nazi: "He just happens to be a little eccentric. Most geniuses are." (Be advised: the Soup Man travels in summer months in search of new recipes.)

Queens

The Costanza House

Ricky, the obsessed TV fanatic, traces Elaine to the Costanza house using the mailing label on Frank Costanza's *TV Guide*. The address is supposedly 1344 Queens Boulevard in Flushing.

Queensboro Plaza

This is the subway stop where one can pick up the N, the 7, or, according to Kramer, the best gyros in the city ("The Cigar Store Indian"). WNBC weatherman Al Roker, who made a twenty-second cameo appearance in the episode, later told viewers about his three takes: "I was in a New York City subway, but I had to fly to Los Angeles to do it."

Queens College

Jerry and George's alma mater, Queens College, is where the real Jerry actually attended college. Perhaps the school's most visible alumnus, Jerry wore a Queens College hat in "The Barber" and a T-shirt in "The Mango" and "The Pool Guy."

LaGuardia Airport

One of two New York City terminals, it's where Jerry and Elaine are routed in "The Airport." It is also the setting for "The Diplomats Club," where Jerry has a rendezvous with a supermodel and Kramer gets in over his head gambling with a Texan on arrivals. George says the best way to get there from Manhattan is the Grand Central Parkway to the Van Wyck Expressway in "The Airport."

John F. Kennedy International Airport

New York City's other terminal, it was Jerry and Elaine's original destination in "The Airport." Jerry says George once made it from Jerry's apartment (West 81st Street) to Kennedy in twenty minutes; trying to impress a woman, George revised the story to fifteen minutes ("The Bubble Boy").

Shea Stadium

Home of the New York Mets, Shea Stadium was also the site of the June 14, 1987, spitting incident, in which Kramer and Newman faced the conse-

Things Were Shakin' All Around

Although they were ensconced in what Billy Joel might call a "New York state of mind," the gang at *Seinfeld* definitely knew they were in Los Angeles when an early 1994 earthquake rocked the *Seinfeld* stage at CBS's Studio City, where the program is filmed.

Beams from the stage were pushed through the walls, executives said, and even though the sets were not damaged much, the crew could not move them because the stage underneath was too unstable. NBC was forced to show reruns during the all-important February sweeps period. But compared to the pain and devastation faced by other victims of the quake, everyone agreed the *Seinfeld* set damage was a relatively minor loss.

quences of taunting baseball players ("The Boyfriend").

The USTA National Tennis Center

Seen every summer as the site of the U.S. Open, this is where Jerry meets a beautiful lineswoman and George is caught on camera eating a hot fudge sundae without a napkin. Kramer breaks the age barrier here as tennis's first "ball man" ("The Lip Reader").

The Bronx

Yankee Stadium

The House That Ruth Built, Yankee Stadium in the Bronx is where George works as assistant to the traveling secretary. Prior to his landing the job, Elaine was ejected (twice) from the stadium for wearing an Orioles cap in club-owner George Steinbrenner's box ("The Letter"). Jerry also meets Miss Rhode Island at the park in "The Chaperone."

Brooklyn

Coney Island

Jerry takes a subway to Coney Island to pick up his stolen car at the pound, but hits it off with a naked Mets fan and instead spends the day at the amusement park and Nathan's ("The Subway").

The Kings of Queens

If it is possible to truly understand Jerry and George, one must start with their old neighborhood in northeast Queens. Only a few miles from Manhattan on the map, Queens is psychologically light-years away from that bustling metropolis. Queens, New York's "bedroom borough," is a diverse mixture of races and nationalities, where George says the life expectancy is seventy-three.

We turned to *Newsday*'s Queens reporter and columnist, Joe Queen, to give us a better picture of life in the land of Seinfelds and Costanzas.

What is your column, "Queen's Queens," all about?

It's basically a column about Queens. I try to get into some of the weirdness that goes on in Queens. Queens is the center of weirdness in the universe. I mean there's something that attracts that sort of element here. Everything from UFOs supposedly landing in Kissena Park to just the weirdos who sort of wander into our office at the newspaper.

Do you notice any similarities between Jerry's and George's parents and genuine Queens people?

Actually there are a lot of them. Especially in the way they talk. Jerry doesn't hide his disdain for Newman—if you listen to Queens people, they usually don't hide the fact whether they like you or not. When you talk to them, you can usually tell right away. They're real straightforward, as opposed to the kissy-kissy type people in Manhattan. . . . People in Queens also tend to talk loud. You know, when you have an argument in Queens it isn't necessarily about throwing facts back and forth—its about who can shout louder.

That sounds like the Costanzas and the Seinfelds. Did you have parents like them on your block when you were growing up?

Actually there were a whole bunch who were sort of like them but not exactly like them. They really are caricatures, like where you take all the worst parts of all of them and roll them into one. You would have them.

Both of New York's airports are in Queens. What impact does that have on the people who live there?

Well, the airports pretty much are Queens. One of the reasons why I think everyone talks so loud is because you have the damn planes coming overhead. You know, if you're not getting the planes from LaGuardia, you're getting them from Kennedy, and in some places you're getting them from both.

Is it possible to make it from West 81st Street to Kennedy Airport in fifteen minutes, as George claims?

Yes, but only at three o'clock in the morning.

According to *Seinfeld*, the best gyros in town are sold on the platform at the Queensboro Plaza subway station. Have you ever seen any gyro vendors there?

No.

Would you recommend anybody eat a gyro sold on the platform?

I wouldn't recommend they eat *anything* sold on the platform.

What does it mean to have the Jerry Seinfeld character represent Queens?

Well, it's better than having Archie Bunker. When everyone thinks of Queens, they think of Archie Bunker, and unfortunately, The Nanny. When you stop and think about it, for all the caricatures that they do on *Seinfeld*, that nanny is worse. Then there was *Northern Exposure*. Dr. Joel Fleishman was from Flushing and went to Bronx Science just like I did. There are a lot of shows that have Queens angles.

Is that because a lot of writers come out of Queens?

Exactly. It's gotta be. Because when you stop to think about it, there's really no sex appeal to Queens. Queens is a place where real people come from—but it's also a center of weirdness. Weird things happen here.

Sein-ing On to the Internet

Need a tape of "The Contest?" Want a list of episode titles to help you label your home-video collection? Wondering where you've seen that guy who played Elaine's boyfriend?

If you have a computer and a modem, chances are help is at your fingertips! *Seinfeld* fans by the thousands are cruising the information superhighway—exchanging notes, swapping tapes, and discussing their favorite scenes. Seems that *Seinfeld* fans, like thousands of other special-interest groups, have made their mark in cyberspace.

The main source of information is the *Seinfeld* "bulletin board" on the Usenet, alt.tv.seinfeld, which is essentially a menu of various subjects "posted" by fans. Topics in the bulletin board usually include reactions to the current episode, Jerry sightings, gossip, favorite lines, and *Seinfeld*-related news.

Although the quality of the bulletin board has gone downhill in recent years (due to incessant advertising for porn sites and get-rich-quick schemes), one can still find some interesting conversation threads here.

Unlike the bulletin board, which the user must actively access, fans can also get themselves on *Seinfeld*-related mailing lists and get the news delivered via e-mail. These lists tend to be smaller in nature, with a few dozen regulars contributing to the discourse. Contact information for getting on

Top Seinfeld-Related Internet Resources

Seinfeld Bulletin Board

Use your local news reader to subscribe to: alt.tv.seinfeld. Choose from a selection of Seinfeld-related topics.

World Wide Web

A search of any good Web search engine will yield dozens of Seinfeld-related Web sites, of varying quality. Some of the best include:

NBC

http://www.nbc.com/tvcentral/shows/seinfeld/index.html

Contains: Star biographies, pictures, transcripts of chats, press information, special events and e-mail links.

Sony

http://www.spe.sony.com/tv/shows/seinfeld/index.html

Contains: Virtual reality tours of Jerry's apartment and Monk's Diner, biographies, photos, sounds and other features.

Vandelay Industries Archive

http://www.cs.cmu.edu/afs/cs/user/vernon/www/vandelay/index.html

Contains: A database of Seinfeld information from the Vandelay Industries fan club (see page 193), including episode guide, frequently asked questions, and other interesting information.

Kenny Kramer's Home Page

http://www.bway.net/~kramer/home.html

Contains: The world according to "The Real Kramer," including personal photos, anecdotes about *Seinfeld*'s creators, merchandise, and information about Kramer's world-famous New York City Reality Tour.

the mailing list changes. Browse through the Usenet bulletin board to find out who the current administrator is.

Bulletin-board users, mailing list readers, and mailing list subscribers will find loads of interesting information and can meet *Seinfeld* fans from all over the world. New users should check them out for a few days before making a contribution (or "post"), just to make sure what is acceptable and what has been covered already. Although these services are free, users should check with their Internet service providers to see what charges apply for accessing them.

Of course, the World Wide Web has exploded as a source of *Seinfeld* information. Dedicated fans have created dozens of unofficial sites honoring their favorite show. These sites often contain text, sounds, pictures, and other material to browse through. In addition, most of these sites are linked to each other, making it easy to surf from one site to another.

Addresses for *Seinfeld*-related sites can be found on any Web directory (the best is http://www.yahoo.com) or on the alt.tv.seinfeld bulletin board. A little hunting will reveal a wide array of material, all available for downloading and printing: news, episode guides, lists of funny lines, amateur-written scripts, sounds, and photo galleries of the stars.

The subject of the Internet has not been brought up much on *Seinfeld*. That's not too surprising, considering Jerry's own computer has only been seen turned on once or twice in nine seasons! On the show, trying to convince Jerry to get on the Net (and buy a computer) George tells his friend he can use a new PC to "check porn and stock quotes" ("The Serenity Now"). Even Kramer checks into the Internet regularly and keeps track of the comedy scene ("I read on the Internet that Bania *killed*!" he said in "The Butter Shave.")

In real life, it's doubtful that Jerry spends much time, if any, surfing the Internet. "I don't want to go online," Jerry once quipped in *Esquire*. "I've waited on line, I've been in lines. I'm not interested in going online."

You never know who you'll meet on the Internet. However, you should know there are a number of impostors out there, including a couple of "Jerry Seinfelds!"

Vandelay Industries: More Than Just Latex

When a dozen fans began discussing a new show called *Seinfeld*, they probably didn't realize what would become of the show—or their efforts. Since the early nineties, the show has obviously become a ratings juggernaut. And the group, which took the name of Vandelay Industries (the made-up latex company at which George claims he applied for a sales position), started an electronic mailing list that now links more than six hundred diehard *Seinfeld* fans around the world.

Originally, Kramer was the group's favorite character. The group even nominated him for president, recalls original member Donna Tschetter, because he had the best qualities a leader could have: "honesty, independence, and a clear vision of how things were."

At the time, a friend of Tschetter's was printing T-shirts for Jerry Brown's presidential campaign. But after the drive fizzled, Tschetter and her friends converted the design to "Kramer for President" and sent one to Jerry Seinfeld. "Jerry loved it!" Tschetter said. "He framed it and hung it on the wall, and soon after that I received a call from the *Seinfeld* office."

A line producer then suggested the group come up with more ideas and submit them to Castle Rock Entertainment, which produces the show, for licensing approval. The group came up with a number of designs, including "The Kramer" (the best seller), "Queen of the Castle," "My Cubans," "Cantstandya," and "Master of My Domain."

Soon after, the group was printing bumper stickers, with famous *Seinfeld* slogans like "Gotta Love the Sein," which led to stories of VI members being followed for blocks by other fans demanding to know where they got the stickers.

In one of the club's wackier moments, members created a persona for "Art Vandelay," got him a Social Security Number and a charge card, and put him on lots of mailing lists. The club also collected money for flood relief and sent a check out in the Vandelay Industries name a couple of summers ago.

Original members are spread out all across the United States. The group even managed to get together for one of Jerry's stand-up shows and a filming of *Seinfeld*.

Now, the only remnants of the fan club is the VI mailing list, said Tschetter.

Epilogue:

All I Really Need to Know I Learned From Watching *Seinfeld*
or
Seinfeld's Little Instruction Book

These days, bookstores are flooded with paperback books offering self-help, life lessons, and miscellaneous spiritual enlightenment. But for fans of Jerry, George, Elaine, and Kramer, rules for living are filtered through the cathode ray tube. This despite a strict writers' code that stipulates "no hugging, no learning." So for all those whose thirty-minute sessions have helped them be psychologically prepared to deal with bad haircuts, party etiquette, and re-gifters, I present these ten *Seinfeld* statutes:

1. Remember to say "thank you."

Not thanking someone for a favor can have disastrous results, as both

Jerry and his father have learned. In "The Face Painter," Jerry's refusal to give a "day-after thank you" to Alec Berg (the guy with the "John Houseman name") cost him tickets to a Rangers playoff game. In "The Cadillac," Morty forgot to thank Sol, a neighbor, for an aisle seat at a Freddy Roman show. The man held a grudge and voted to impeach Morty from the condo board.

2. Be nice to your mailman.

Moving the nation's mail is no easy task. In "The Old Man," Newman explains why his job at the post office gets him so edgy: "The mail never stops. Every day it piles up more and more and more and you gotta get it out. But the more you get out, the more it keeps coming in. And then the barcode reader breaks. And then it's Publishers Clearing House day!" Fortunately, most of the folks who collect, sort, and deliver our nation's mail are friendlier than Jerry's explosive neighbor. So next time you see your letter carrier, give him or her a smile, a wave, and maybe even a kiss hello. After all, as Newman said, "When you control the mail, you control . . . information!"

3. You can still get a great parking spot if you apply yourself.

According to George Costanza, paying for parking is like going to a prostitute. Why pay for something when you can get it for free? If you're parallel parking, remember to back in ("The Parking Space"). If you're at the shopping mall, remember where you leave the car!

4. Try doing the opposite.

Are you tired of your routine? Do things never seem to work out for you? Try changing your lunch order, the way you drive, or how you approach members of the opposite sex. As Jerry pointed out to George, "If every instinct you have is wrong, then the opposite would have to be right" ("The Opposite").

5. Soup is a meal.

Soup is not just good food, it can be worth an Armani suit ("The Soup"). And if that soup is really, really good, you'll even dump your significant other to get it ("The Soup Nazi").

6. Look to the cookie.

In these times of ethnic and political divisiveness, we can all take a lesson from the black-and-white cookie featured in "The Dinner Party": two races of flavor living together in harmony.

7. Lie, lie, lie!

If you're ever faced with telling the truth or telling a lie in order to gain . . . lie, lie, lie! If necessary, get a conspirator to help you come up with "the best possible lie." "Remember," George reveals in "The Beard," "it's not a lie if you believe it."

8. If you are ever lucky enough to date a woman who looks like Teri Hatcher, don't even think about asking if her breasts are fake.

You might, however, send an accomplice into the health club sauna to find out for you ("The Implant").

9. Tub is love.

The surest way to get a date out of your apartment is to have a dirty bathroom. Elaine confirms this theory in "The Phone Message," when she complains: "I once broke up with a guy 'cause he didn't keep his bathroom